"What a wonderful way to tell stories! These are soul stories, indeed, for the cowpoke in all of us who loves these plains and rolling hills, whether we have ever herded cattle or even ridden a horse or not. Marshall Veal reminds us of a life where feeling free and working hard are still reckoned to belong together."

— Alan Parry, University of Calgary; author of *A Universe of Stories.*

"Already an accomplished singer-songwriter, Marshall Veal adds a surprising new dimension to his repertoire with this debut collection of poetry. From whimsical bagatelles to broad narratives and intimate flashes of detail, he roams the poetic spectrum as his indian and cowboy heroes roamed the once-open range. By turns dramatic, reflective, elegiac and humorous, Marshall Veal maps new territory here – where the mystic East meets the stoic West – and leaves the reader with a vision of unity that encompasses the great men of Western history, dreams of the future, and the ever-present land itself. This is a book with unusual depth, clarity, and heart."

– Max Foran, University of Calgary;
author of *The Madonna List.*

"When you are a rancher,
if you grow grass everything else is secondary."

– Lonnie Jones

Who has seen the West

poems, songs & reflections

Marshall Veal

⊰ Centennial Edition ⊱

SAUDARA MUSIC

2005

Cover design by Marshall Veal and Robert Sawatzky
Photography by Sagara
Production: Bunne, Rabbit & Herr Productions

Published by:
SAUDARA MUSIC
Box 429 – 1917 West 4th Avenue
Vancouver B.C., V6J 1M7, Canada

General & author inquiries: www.marshallveal.net

Note for Librarians: A cataloguing record for this book is available from Library and Archives Canada at www.collectionscanada.ca/amicus/index-e.html
ISBN 1-4120-5971-2

Printed in Victoria, BC, Canada. Printed on paper with minimum 30% recycled fibre.
Trafford's print shop runs on "green energy" from solar, wind and other environmentally-friendly power sources.

Offices in Canada, USA, Ireland and UK
Book sales for North America and international:
Trafford Publishing, 6E–2333 Government St.,
Victoria, BC V8T 4P4 CANADA
phone 250 383 6864 (toll-free 1 888 232 4444)
fax 250 383 6804; email to orders@trafford.com
Book sales in Europe:
Trafford Publishing (UK) Limited, 9 Park End Street, 2nd Floor
Oxford, UK OX1 1HH UNITED KINGDOM
phone 44 (0)1865 722 113 (local rate 0845 230 9601)
facsimile 44 (0)1865 722 868; info.uk@trafford.com
Order online at:
trafford.com/05-0872

10 9 8 7 6 5 4 3 2

For my mother, June Harrison, the first poet
I ever encountered; and for my father, Art Veal,
a prairie kid who found just the right gal.
Their love story would give birth to future storytellers.

Acknowledgements

My thanks to the poets, pickers, dreamers, seekers, and storytellers...the give and take is inspiring; and to all who support the poetic arts...may they also feel the poetry within; to Doris Bircham, Alan Parry and Max Foran, for their inspirations and affirmations; to Avi Cohen, Jon Kabat-Zinn, Liz Neil, Naya Kee, Alan & Elke Parry, Lee Shedden, Heather MacEwan Foran, my sister Marianna, Joe Morin, and the many more who have encouraged me along the way; to Fran Seward (FJS), for her poetic collaboration and companionship; to Dave Ander at Freedom Ranch; to Lucas Hille & M.N. for collaboration on 'San Diego'; to Sagara, for her wonderful photography & help with 'Lonesome Cowgirl'; to my daughter Tara, and her husband Eric; to my granddaughters Mie and Aisling...may they someday read and wonder...as I have...how our ancestors ever built a life on the prairies; to folks at the ol' Black Diamond Hotel; to all who help run Poetry Gatherings & Folk Fests across the West; to Kim Taylor, and Lonnie Jones, for their permissions; to Robert Sawatzky, for his friendship and collaboration; to cited authors, for their resilient work; to the folks at Trafford; to folks who feature independent artists in retail across the West; and to Sophia...my favourite Chihuahua. Thank you all, for the wonderful stories.

Contents

Peoples Who Came First

The Old West

Cowboys, Cowgirls 'n Poets

Outlaws, Heroes 'n Such

This Western Romance

Places Of The Heart

Now And Zen In The West

The Enduring West

Epilogue

Preface

When does a poem become a song…or a song a poem? Or must the twain forever be separated? Sorry, Shania.

At 5:30 in the morning in a casa on the plains… lingering over wine, music and poetry, an early autumn evening having eased almost imperceptibly into a new day…that's when poems and songs may intermingle, and all becomes one. And Eliza's soulful songs seem to stroke and caress our weary but contented brow.

In these pages you'll find species allowed to mingle…poems, songs, dreams, visions, reflections and direct quotations… all speaking their metaphors, all adapting to the form of poetic verse. Music symbols are used to denote the species origin of a piece as a song (with choruses denoted in italics). And music for the songs, in the form of simple chord charts…or more detailed charts, may (theoretically) be supplied, for a few shekels… upon request. In this book, the music is left to imagination, while the lyric unfolds the story. If you are moved by a lyric, you are welcome to contact us about the music.

When does East become West, or West become East? And when they meet, do they ever find themselves… in each other?

Some of these verses speak of open range and open mind… sometimes synonymously… even in one breath. And you may find verses which evoke memories of some of those, whatever race or color, who knew the open range…and who struggled to understand with clear vision and open mind…the changes confronting them…as do many of us in the West today. I have found it inspiring, and surprisingly entertaining, in mixing metaphors of East and West, to discover parallels in the wisdom and humour of the old West and older East, as exemplified in cowboy poetry and zen poetry. I have also found some of the most moving and poetic reflections on the West to have been spoken by great chiefs, including Big Bear, Crowfoot, Joseph, Poundmaker, Red Cloud, Seattle, and Sitting Bull… some of whose words and images, thanks to the resourceful work of preceding authors, I have found and included in these verses. Perhaps these days, and in the future, it will take an open mind to still find the freedom and inspiration ...of life lived on a truly open range.

The last piece written for this book... 'In The Dreaming West'... was written in the last week of 2005. On reading Sharon Butala's 'Lilac Moon', and her recounting of the re-introduction of Plains Bison at Old Man On His Back, another story which continues to haunt me, the massacre of Bald Eagles by poachers on the West coast...occurring recently...and season after season... flooded in again, and led somehow to an integration of inverse themes in an obscure yet culminating poem. And finally, as much of what is found here involves music...let it be said, that the West will surely always be heard as much as it may be seen.

Who Has Seen The West –

is a collection which reflects a lifetime's interest in the North American West...from Manitoba to the Pacific, from the Yellowhead to south of the Rio Grande. And though we had intended to publish in time for the summer 2005 Centennial Celebrations of Alberta and Saskatchewan...it was apparently not to be. However, we are confident of publishing sometime well before the next Centennial rolls around. If poetry can be timeless... perhaps this collection will survive through and beyond 2105...to future Centennials!

What you may find in this collection, then, is an open range of moods and timbres... and above all....an acknowledgement and love of awesome territory, history, peoples, and a cultural melange...the meta story which we call...The West. And each one of us, after all, may be its storyteller!

December 31, 2005

Marshall

Who has seen the West

Glimpses

"….With the vision
Of the eagle."

Sunrise

I awaken
The beauty of sunrise
Greets me
Glorious golden colours
Invite me
Again
To open my eyes
As if
For the first time
I awaken

Riding With Eagle Feather

While dreaming
I find various small feathers
On the ground
Which seem like clues
To a path I must follow
And they lead me at last
To one large eagle feather
Which I pick up and grasp in awe
When suddenly
The feather accelerates
In an upward motion
Like a rocket
And as I affirm my grasp
I am carried upward
At great speed
The wind against my face
Into the sky
From where I can see
At great distance
And observe
In wonderment
Many things –
With the vision
Of the eagle

On Daniel Point

In the dream seven years ago
Or was it eight –
I dreamed I should live in Pender Harbour
That's all in essence I recall
But the dream was lucid
And stark in its simplicity
Like an Oracle's prophecy
But what of a harbour, for a landlubber like me?

I wasn't even sure where Pender Harbour was
Or even if it was –
Perhaps somewhere on the coast – brilliant!
Aha – something to do with Pender Island
But once cleverly locating its geographic nexus
I found it to be within reasonable reach
And so determined just to go and visit
Without further need of such formidable research

On our first visit seven years ago
Or was it six –
We inadvertently ascended Daniel Point
Not knowing it's name or that we were There
We found telltale signs of intended development
Before it was all bought up by people
With almost enough dough to kiss the world
goodbye
As they too follow their most hallowed dreams

And climbing the crest of this promontory
Whatever was its name –
This broad breathtaking panoramic view
Of atmosphere sublime
Above Malaspina Strait where one can dream
In an open expanse so majestic and serene
Where eagle soars overhead
And dreams a dream like yours and mine

Of islands in the distance
Texada, Vancouver, and on –
These islands in the mist
Islands of possibility and hope
The self as an island
A self within the whole
A larger sense of being
In self – world – belonging – whole

Returning again this summer at last
Five years since a second visit –
I continue to ponder on the dream
And why I still feel like a visitor
Within my own spiritual home
Yet in these past few weeks
Camping in Pender harbour
There is a firmer sense of place

A sense that I now live
In Pender Harbour –
And that she lives in me
And the meaning of the dream I suppose
Is in finding serenity
Serenity of place – serenity of mind
And as the eagle soars
Now so do I

Will I live in Pender Harbour
Lock, stock and barrel? –
I may not know now
But I do now know
That there is a harbour
Of serenity within
A safe harbour in which to dream
Where the work of soul may carry on

The Eagle And The Bull

In the dream I could see this young bull
So full of life
But left alone in a dangerous world
Out of its natural environment
And somehow... I wanted to protect it

Finally...I looked up in the sky
And saw an eagle
Returning to a nesting place
So I told the bull...look...
Do you want to go visit the eagle?

So the young bull
Without speaking
Said yes...
And then he suddenly flew up
To be with the eagle

And after a while the eagle flew down
To tell me that the bull had died
And that on his death bed...
Though he hadn't reached
the fifth level of heaven
He was free...and in a better place

Dream Of Power

Late into the night
Even by dawn's first light
As I lay sleeping
I heard a voice
The voice of a bird
Not of a man
Was it Crow, Eagle
Or Raven ?
I believe it was Raven
Who spoke to me, and
Repeated at regular short intervals…
One word only…
In it's croaky voice it said:
"Power…Power…Power…
Power…Power…Power"
Six times I believe…
Until it ceased

I awoke, later on
And wondering at what I'd heard –
Is this my time of awakening
To my connection with
A power spirit
My own power within
The power of creativity
The shamanic touch
The life force in all being ?
Whatever it is
Whomever spoke
It is for me to recognise
For as it spoke to me alone
No one else shall interpret my life to me
That is for me now
And this is the realisation
Of a spiritual power

The Oceans Are Turning Blue

The oceans are turning blue, my friend
The oceans are turning so blue
So what are we gonna' do my friend
For the oceans are feeling so blue

And where will the salmon run, my friend
Where will the salmon run
When their rivers run hot and polluted my friend
Oh where will the salmon run

And where have the cod fish gone, my friend
Where have the cod fish gone
Have they gone the way of the Inca gold
Oh where have the cod fish gone

And how could the lakes all die, my friend
How could the lake waters die
If we fill them with smog and motor boat oil
Oh that's how the lake waters die

And someday the whales may be gone, my friend
Someday the whales may be gone
If we don't turn the tide around my friend
Someday the whales will be gone

And a hard rain's gonna' come down, my friend
You know whatever goes up will come down
If we keep pumpin' poisin to the sky my friend
You know the hard rain's gonna come down

And the oceans are turning blue, my friend
The oceans are feeling the blues
Now it's down to me and you my friend
For the oceans are turning so blue

Teachings of The Eagle Spirit

one

A baby eagle…an eaglet
Appeared last night to me
In a dream
Spontaneous
Unpredictable
Joyous
Delighting me
As it jumped all over our bed
I couldn't at first name it
Control it or predict it
Even though at first I wanted to
It seemed to have it's own
Energy…destiny…and will
"Isn't it cute"…I said over again
And through this vision I know
It's all part of me –
Wishing and capable of being
Joyous, creative
And free

two

Standing in my parlour
In company, I dream
When suddenly
A full grown eagle appears
And lands with great flourish
Upon my right shoulder
Where it nobly sits –
I am in awe of its power
A sense of honour and wonder

In the intensity of the moment
When – without warning
The eagle relieves itself upon my shoulder
I am aghast – and then amazed
My pride and composure
Sullied, then suspended
And corrected
A lesson in pride
Passion
And the acceptance of what is

three

I stand in the kitchen
Of my boyhood home
In my dream I see
A bald eagle in our backyard
Through the open kitchen door
He looks at me
He begins to trundle toward me
Into the house
I stand in awe and fear
Of his power and his intent
He wants to be fed
There is no doubt
He will not be denied
I see it in his eyes
And in every part of me
I feed him meat from my hand
And it is so –
Honour the passions
Do not deny that they are you

four

The eagle beckons me
To let go
And jump down from the cliff
Into brooding waters below
Where earlier downstream
I had helplessly witnessed
My lover pulled down
Beneath the waters
By alien beings –
I dare not go
I won't let go
Where would I be
In such depths
As I have never known?
To jump may have meant
Letting go of the life I know
Or following a path not truly my own
I was not ready for that
No, but to let my lover go

Sea Shore Song ♪

Sleeping down by the sea shore
morning comes like the day before
Seagulls waking watching o'er
take their early inventory

Evening fire light along the shore
kiss the sky like the night before
Blending into the deep beyond
coming back with wings of dawn

So we live our timeless dream
set our sails and find...our dream ♪

The Natural West

"….Why is a hawk?…'

Adams River Uprising

Adams River Uprising, October 18, 2002:
The Sockeye are totally committed –
We're gonna' do this river
We're gonna' sink or spawn
We're on a holy mission
People…listen to our song

We are the Sockeye Salmon
We are wild and free…are you?
We will follow Mother Nature
As we always do…will you?
We only follow our dream…do you?
This is all we know… and all we can tell you

We don't blame or denigrate you
Because you may forget your nature
We don't possess your cerebral powers
The so called evolutionary advantage
Still, we know that though you fear
Our hope is that you too will remember to dream

Oh please all brothers and sisters
Listen to our song
May we all live long together
And every voice find its own natural song
For more than any one selfish ambition
Mother Earth needs our love and attention

Adams River Uprising, October 2002:
The salmon are totally committed
They're gonna' follow through –
We're gonna' run this river
For we are the Sockeye Salmon
We are wild and almost free...are you?

Horse Heaven Hills

Horses came to this rugged new land
Across those wild Atlantic seas
With the blood in our veins primed
By the Asian steppes and Spanish plains
We took to it well here and what is more
We went where no man could take us
And discovered all for ourselves
Freedom in these Horse Heaven Hills

Up here in the high country
Way out by the Toppenish Ridge
Out here in the sage and short grass
And the rambling mountain peaks
Us Horses went our own way
Liberated, wild and free
And discovered all for ourselves
A haven in these Horse Heaven Hills

The Oregon Trail soon opened up
A land of such unspoiled expanse
As word spread fast of an open range
And a future full of promise
But that was already long after
We had broken free of human masters
And discovered all for ourselves
These magnificent Horse Heaven Hills

Now desert motels rodeos and truck stops
Dot and cross the land like punctuation marks
Fences Wal-Marts and honky tonks
The gifts of civilization never seem to stop
But way out here on the Chilcotin and beyond
The Lost Horse Plateau and the Owyhee Range
Something men don't control still remains
Where wild spirits rule these Horse Heaven Hills

For they may ride rope and brand me
They may lasso corral and stampede me
They may buy sell and trade me
But will they ever really know me?
As history is my witness
As empires rise and fall
My spirit will always break free
And leave them to their ills
And I, to my Horse Heaven Hills

Birds And Trees

Birds and trees
How were they so made –
For each other?

High Wire Act

Our spider friends –
   Guess who we learned
      Tightrope walking from?

Eagles ♪

The winds of december
always bring more than the rain
Up here on the northwest coast
when it's winter again
The mighty Pacific
thunders and breaks on the shore
And by the time it's december
the eagle has landed once more

They fly from Alaska
the Yukon and northern BC
To the quiet river valleys
where the salmon still come to breed
From the Skagit to the Squamish
they'll be comin' through the mist and the rain
And by the time it's december
the eagle has landed again

How many seasons
how many thousands of times
How do they manage
how do they ever survive
And if we could ask them
the only answer they'd give
For the reason they fly
is the same as the reason we live

And they fly
that they may live
And they live
that they may dream
And we dream
of being free
To fly on the wings of the wind
Like eagles on the wings of the wind

Now the old Squamish Chief
stands still like a mountain of stone
His soul is all weathered
by the years of the wind and snow
But every december
I swear I see a smile on his face
When his old friend the eagle
comes back to see him again

And they fly
that they may live
And they live
that they may dream
And we dream
of being free
To fly on the wings of the wind
Like eagles on the wings of the wind ♪

Flying Home

Sunset –
The sudden call from high overhead
Out of the evening sky
Ravens in formation
Flying on by
And calling out
As they fly home
To their long awaited evening rest
Somewhere deep in this dark rainforest

They travel from the east
After a full day
Of living, scavenging
And mischievous adventure
Raiding other territories –
They are flying home
And calling out their high altitude song
They call to each other joyously
And as if, to the world below

These dark and vivid warriors
Like crisp black shadows
On a wayang canvas
Of perfumed purple sky –
We are pilgrims, they cry
We are coming through
Today we have lived well
Tomorrow we may well die
'And tonight, we are flying home

The Mating

I turn my gaze
To my left
And putting down my book
To reach again
For my whiskeyed coffee cup
When suddenly
In mid-air
Just above the table top
Two dragonflies – there

In an instant
Copulating
In a dizzying dance
A brief exchange
A brief romance
And then
Just as suddenly
They separate – and fly
In varying directions

I try
But cannot follow
Until they are gone to me
And from each other
I return to my writing
A witness – participant
In this momentary
Confluence
Of being

The Great Blue Heron

She wafts her great wings
In rhythmic slow waves
Just skimming along the shoreline
Then rapidly ascending
Into a sudden flourishing finale
She alights upon a chosen rooftop
And comes to rest upon the crest
Of your multi-million dollar love nest
Overlooking Her Burrard Inlet –
Do you know She has arrived?
Do you feel Her presence – inside
A sense of honour
Noblesse oblige twice born
In your privilege of hosting Her? –
Well if you do, then so you should

For She is indeed a regal figure
The latest of her lineage
And of course
Like countless generations
Of Her kind before
This is Her higher ground
This is Her shore
And you are a recent arrival –
And your great vaulted roof
Another kind of welcome throne
From which She surveys Her kingdom –
And only as we honour each other
Will the kingdom survive
And the Great Blue Heron
Deign to be our gracious guide

Fire In The Canyon ♪

Fire in the canyon
smoke in the hills
All hell's broken loose
and the flames are spreadin' still
And high on the mountain
there's no sign of rain
It's fire in the canyon
and the devil is to blame

Summer came early
on the high chaparall
Winter stayed so long
spring didn't come at all
'Til sagebrush and timber
were burnt by the sun
And high in the pines
the damage was done

Through june and july
and day after day
A hundred degrees
and more in the shade
And when lightning did strike
and a spark did ignite
By the time it was august
we were all on the run

Well the crews fought hard
through the night and the day
'Til the people were told
you'd best evacuate
And the ranches and homes
that stood in the way
Were soon swept away
in the heat of the blaze

For two weeks and more
we battled the flames
'Til all we could do
was to pray for the rain
Then a north wind blew in
and Salmon Arm was saved
But the scars on the hills
told the price that was paid

Fire in the canyon
smoke in the hills
All hell's broken loose
and the flames are spreadin' still
And high on the mountain
there's no sign of rain
It's fire in the canyon
and the devil is to blame ♪

How To Tell The Difference

How do you tell the difference
between an animal and a man?
Well if you're from outer space pardner
this poem will help you so you can

You see an animal can relax
at the drop of a hat
Unless threatened by beast
or bothered by man

Animals don't lie awake at night
worryin' about what might have been
They don't even sweat the big stuff
and they never plot and scheme

Animals always tell the truth
they tell it like it is
Unless they know it's a game
or survival depends on it

Animals don't make excuses
they just give it all they've got
How often do you see that anymore
amongst the human lot

Animals don't mistreat each other
or abuse themselves for long
They don't smoke, drink and gamble
or write those crazy country songs

Animals rarely waste energy
doing futile silly things
It's known that mules and sloths are experts
on subjects such as this

Animals may fight, rage
compete and disagree
But they rarely hold a grudge
or let it fester there for years

Animals are quick to let you know
exactly where they stand
They don't lead you on
or pretend to be what they ain't

Animals will find a way
to solve most any problem soon
And they won't keep on tryin' and frettin'
to shoot beyond the moon

Animals do not misguide, mistreat
or misinform their young
They teach 'em without punishment
to know what's right and wrong

They do not teach 'em to feel
shame, guilt or neglect
They make great parents naturally
and they always do their best

Animals don't pollute, damage
or disfigure Mother Earth
They take only what they need
and they seem to know its worth

Animals act spontaneously
and they always follow their senses
They don't live in denial
behind big white picket fences

Animals live according
to the laws of Mother Nature
They don't try to dominate
manipulate and control her

Animals seem to live
with respect for their maker
They don't try to buy and sell
or simply overtake her

Animals don't try to be perfect
or make a perfect world
And they don't get bored or lazy
unless confined in a zoo

So if you've come from outer space
to take a look around
And you're wondering who's in charge
down on this earthly ground

Well it won't take you long to figure out
which species is the smarter
Then you'll ask the nearest animal
to take you to their leader

Mister Moo ♪

How do you do Mister Moo
how do you do what you do?
I saw you today where the green grass sways
outstanding in your field
When I passed by in the wink of an eye
I thought I could hear you say
My name is Moo how do you do
a moo moo moo to you

Drivin' my car I can go far
under the big blue sky
All of the cows hangin' around
Seem to watch me passing by
I'd like to say have a nice day
and I hope you enjoy the hay
A swish of a tail and it's happy trails
until we meet again

Hey Mister Moo what do you do
when you're feeling blue?
Do you have days when skies are gray
and you'd just like to get away?
Down on the farm back in the barn
do you ever want a holiday?
And hay diddle diddle, if the cat plays a fiddle
would you jump right over the moon?

Blacks and whites
and Holsteins too
Jerseys Guernseys
they all say moo
Ask them any old
question at all
And all you're gonna' get
is a cattle call ♪

Party Animals

I tried to get some sleep last night
out on the lone prairie
I bedded down beneath the stars
the better for them to see
My dog barked out at something
then a coyote answered back
Pretty soon every canine in the county
was a-gettin' in on the act

Well they began a-howlin'
'til they were goin' full throttle
My dog got so carried away
why she even tried to yodel
And when every hound for miles around
had joined in on the racket
Well it seemed like one big convention
of wolf packs a-goin' at it

Well they'd stop every so often
and I would thank the gods
Then I'd turn over in my bedroll
and start a-sawin' on them logs
But then some mangey old cow
would give a lonesome cattle call
And then the whole damn bunch
would go and start all over again and all

So I finally figured why fight 'em
I might as well join in
So I popped the cork on my whiskey flask
and I began to sing
Well I sang every damn song I knew
out there among the stars
And them critters seemed to like it
for they sang along for hours

Well the party went on all night long
until the break of dawn
When my whiskey jug was empty
and I'd run clean out of songs
Then everything got so quiet
like the world was fast asleep
And I figured in those few moments
I'd found eternity

And then before I knew it
the dawn had turned to day
My old dog licked me on the kisser
as if she had to say
That every dog's got to have its day
and I can see she's not far wrong
Because out here on the prairies
they like to party all night long

Nuggets

Eyes of the dragonfly –
Glistening turquoise nuggets
In the summer sun

Early Ones

Does the early worm
Knowingly offer itself
To the early bird?

The Cedar

The great cedar stands
In silent regal splendour
At the edge of the dark forest
Her velvet needles draped
Like the many-layered gown
Of the emperor's favoured consort –
How much
And how many years
Has she seen
Beyond
What I can know
And yet –
I see her clearly
By moonlight

The Poplars

Standing there
Across the street
From this coffee shop window
Where I sit looking out
Into eternity
The poplars –
As the wind picks up
And catches the leaves
Inviting them to dance
Instead of just
Hanging there
Waiting like victims
To fall
From cold branches
Like scaffolds
On poplar trees
In autumn

The Snowy Owl

Late autumn moonlight –
The snowy owl
Pretending to be a branch

In winter –
The snowy owl
Seems so wise

Like an old monk
In mid-winter
The snowy owl sits still – until

Why Is A Hawk?

Why is a hawk?
And where did it come from?
Did someone somewhere one day decide
We need some hawks?

Or is it simply that
There are hawks because there are mice?
We may never really know
But wouldn't it be so very nice

If we all could really see
And deeply feel
The interrelationship
Of all living things?

Peoples Who Came First

"….Who were these people…
who walked upon water and land…"

Legends In Petroglyphs

Who were these people
who crossed the Bering Sea
Who were these people
who wanted to be free

Who were these people
who walked upon water and land
From the midnight sun circle
to the burning desert sand

And was it just a matter of degree
that turned their skin to bronze
Or made them travel eastward
toward the rising sun

The legends of the past
still echo through the years
Recorded in these petroglyphs
these totem poles and caves

The wisdom of a people
carved in wood and stone
The hunger of a people
looking for a home

9 – 11 – 1885

"Now my heart is on the ground
I am dead to my people –
If the government does not come…with help
Before the winter sets in
My band will surely perish"
And so Big Bear reflected in sorrow
On the losses of his people
Just as he had foreseen
In his dream as a boy of twelve
His frightful prescience then
And a lifetime spent in attempts
To avert such an end
His wisdom and integrity
Well known among native peoples
A man who lived according to his visions
Until his first vision became realized
And in the heat of others' many passions
So misunderstood and misinterpreted
And finally at his trial, convicted
By men of lesser vision
On September 11, 1885

"This is our land!
It isn't just a piece of pemmican –
To be cut off and given in little pieces
back to us….It is ours…"
And so Poundmaker spoke
Before…reluctantly

He signed Treaty Six
And then
With the end of the buffalo
And the affairs of the wider world
felt in the consequences of starvation
As all hell broke loose
At Battleford and Cut Knife Hill
Where this man of peace
Could no longer abate
The passions of angered hungry men
With Treaty Six a tattered hypocrisy
Until at his trial on July 4, 1885
He did say thus:
"You did not catch me –
I gave myself up…you have got me
Because I wanted peace"

And for the tormented soul –
The visionary in whom
Conscience is the battleground
Of temperance and desire
Riel sought to remake
The Absolute
According to his image
Of what the Absolute should be
In the wake of the suffering
Of his people – and his own
He followed his vision
As it transformed
And when buffeted by failure

Tailored it to achieve
Acceptance by one and all
Even through Batoche
And prison, trial and conviction
And though outwardly repentant
Yet unbroken in his faith
His Godly mission on earth ended
That 16 November, 1885

And for Crowfoot
The Father of His People
1885 was a year
Of tragedy and affirmation –
The death of his daughter
The imprisonment of Poundmaker
His adopted Cree son
The futility of war as a means to peace
As was Riel's Rebellion
To which Crowfoot was invited
But refused to go along
For he had long foreseen
That resistance to cosmic change is futile
And in his last words he said:
"What is life?
It is as the flash of a firefly in the night
It is as the breath of the buffalo
In the winter time
It is as the little shadow
That runs across the grass
And loses itself in the sunset"

Sitting Bull ♪

The battle soon was over
The war was all but lost
And Sitting Bull alone
Could see what it had cost
So he took the people north
Across the Medicine Line
Where the Great White Mother
Would surely be more kind

They moved onto the land
Called Saskatchewan
This proud and mighty nation
Half starving and undone
In a place called Wood Mountain
East of the Cypress Hills
Guided by a shaman
Seeking only peace

In a land where once the truth
Was known by everyone
And to lie was a thing
In honour never done
Where life was often hard
And punishment was strong
And Nature was the creed
Which guided everyone

But the governments wouldn't listen
Except for Major Walsh
And when all hope was gone
The people headed south
Back to a reservation
Where the government decreed
The Indian war was over
The conquest was complete

The war had finally ended
His vision all but lost
And Sitting Bull alone
Could see what it had cost
And on a cold hard prison floor
The father of the Sioux
Died there just like Jesus
Died for me and you

How can you sell the earth
How can you fence the sky
How can you move a mountain
How can you tell a lie
And who has seen the wind
And who has touched the sky
And who of those among us
Will never have to die ♪

No More Bull

I've been reading more about Sitting Bull of late
I've been somewhat obsessed with his story –
A discovery of something more, of myself,
perhaps?

The whiteman called him the most savage –
And thus he and his people were soon savaged
By the white supremicists of the day

He saw the extermination of the buffalo –
And if he had lived longer he might have seen
The near extinction of eagle, falcon,
elephant and whale

For his was the challenge
of any person of conscience –
Whether to stand tall or to sit idly by
While folly marches on
and sings its righteous song

And what is it then about righteous ingenuity
That renders the world so unfit
For natural life to go on living?

And what is it about the belief in progress
That leads us in a Custer-like charge
To the industrial-strength extinction
of the species?

In 600 years it seems this righteous ingenuity
Has upset the autonomic self-regulation
Of the planet and all her species

In 600 years destroyed –
Aztec, Indian and African Kingdoms
Leaving much of East and West rent, laid bare

In 600 years the printing press
Has documented the extinction of oral traditions
As the chic bookstore eulogizes the biosphere

Yet it wasn't the whiteman who invented war
Or every other human perdition –
For most have existed long before

But a particular genius at reductionism
So upsets, unleashes and creates
A Biochemical Chaos – an ABC of Devolution

Is it our science, politics or our fear
That takes things apart –
Studying the order and abandoning the soul
in a junkyard of discarded conscience?

Sitting Bull faced the full force
Of the whiteman's myopic fury –
And saw the eradication of his world of vision

Standing resolutely until he knew it was done
And trembling at the edge of his extinction –
When that iron trojan horse had finally come
for him

And in the next 600 years –
Will we put our faith in science and/or soul
To rescue us from our selfishness ?

And will each of us face a test of conscience
Like Sitting Bull endured –
When the trojan horse of gaudy progress
comes to beckon to us all

Or may we dedicate ourselves
to a new/old notion of progress
In compassion and understanding –
Where we live here once and for all,
together

It may be ultimately out of our hands
But in our every single action…
Are conscience and compassion alive and well?

Song Of Joseph ♪

"From where the sun stands now
From this moment on
I will fight no more
I will go back home"
No more weapons of war
No more trail of tears
This is a time for peace
And a time to heal

When the great white father
Came to take the land
He sent his sons to take it
He did not understand
That those who live for power
They will never know
The hunger that they feel
Is the hunger of their soul

Hear me oh my people
And all you leaders of men
War can change nothing
If hatred never ends
Then let us sew the earth
With the seeds of love
Until the food of peace we grow
Shall feed everyone

"From where the sun stands now
From this moment on…"
Let us fight no more
Let us live as one
As the sun and moon
Share the sky above
Let us learn to share
Let us learn to love ♪

Peigan Skies ♪

Ridin' south on the eastern slope
Restless feeling in my blood
Thinkin' about our last goodbye
Under the spell of these Peigan skies

Storms roll in as fast as sin
Pincher Creek on the rise again
Crows Nest Pass all deep in snow
Old Man River begins to roar

Storm clouds roll across a troubled mind
Shafts of light pierce the blackened sky
Like a Peigan lance and a warrior's cry
Deep in the heart of this heart of mine

Full moon shines across the midnight sky
Shines so bright you can see for miles
Across the endless midnight miles
So many miles between you and I tonight

Ghosts of the past still dance above
Ancient hills where the buffalo jump
So many sons have come and gone
Northern mystery lives on and on

Will this winter never end
Bad blood end and good begin
Bad blood stands like a great divide
Under the spell of these Peigan skies tonight ♪

Rivers To The Sun

It goes on
Though the buffalo are gone
Though the open range is no more
Still, it goes on

It goes on, my friend
Though the salmon are few
Though their rivers are dirty
It goes on

For as long as there are rivers
The salmon will try to run
And as long as there are skies
The eagle will want to fly

It goes on, my friend
We have our stories of the past
And we all have our scars
But still, it goes on

It goes on, my friend
Though the past has come and gone
New life springs from the ground each day
And so, it goes on

It goes on, my friend
For we are all storytellers
And to be free we can step outside
Those stories which confine us

It goes on, my friend
Let your heart find its own song
Do not cling to the past –
Ancient stories of right and wrong

It goes on, my friend
For life is happening now
And the past is but our stories
Of how things used to be

It goes on, my friend
And as surely as the sun
We are all in this together
All beings equal in being, one

It goes on, my friend
So let your spirit soar
Let your life begin each day
And follow these rivers to the sun

Spirits On The Wind ♪

My home is where the eagles fly
Up in the wild blue sky
Above the silver waters
And the mighty ocean tide
Along the rushing rivers
Where the salmon come again
My home is where the eagles fly
The spirits on the wind

Before the oil tankers
Cut the waters of the whale
And the telephone and the telegraph
Put an end to the buffalo trail
When the people of the forest
And the people of the plains
Looked for wisdom up above
To the spirits on the wind

We have but a short time to walk this earth
We have but a short time upon the land
So little time to understand
Or help our friends
The spirits on the wind

So let us do the best we can
Just like our friends
We're all spirits on the wind ♪

The Old West

.

"....They followed their dreams
And they followed the sun..."

The Buffalo Range

I've travelled down the buffalo range
From Manitoba to the Texas plains
Where buffalo always found their way
In Nature's high domain

I've heard about an open range
From the Yellowhead to the Rio Grande
Where the redman followed the buffalo
To shelter, food and refrain

I've lived out on the northern plains
Where my great grandad once staked a claim
And raised a clan of women and men
All scattered like seeds on the western wind

The wind blows strong across the plains
The coyote howls as if to pray
God keep our home out on the range
Where once the buffalo was king

Oregon Trail ♪

Missouri River
Looks deep and wide
To a poor mid-west farmer
On the eastern side
And with life gettin' harder
Each passing day
Well the Oregon Trail
Seemed to call me by name

Now the 1840's
Were hungry and lean
And prospects were few
For people like me
But 500 dollars
Can buy you a stake
On a wagon train leavin'
By the middle of May

From Westport Landing
Up to old St. Joe
They were packin' it up
Gettin' ready to go
And from all of the stories
How could you tell
There'd be little to choose
Between heaven and hell

2000 miles
And six months of road
If you don't leave in May
You'll die in the snow
Oh the many who travelled
And the many who fell
Gambled all they had
On the Oregon Trail

Stay close to the rivers
As far as you can
Good water's the difference
Between livin' and death
The Kansas and the Blue
And the Platte rivers wind
They'll take you clear out
To the Great Divide

Oh the Indian peoples
I shall not forget
And the many and different
Tribes that we met
We were takin' their land
And their way of life
Though few of us knew
It was so at the time

Then the buffalo scattered
And Red Cloud could see
How his people were falling
To the white man's disease
He was honest enough
Until the government lied
Tell me who is to blame
That so many have died

Oh the Sweetwater Basin
Is barren and dry
But the Mormons will help you
On the other side
And the Snake River country
Seems to wind without end
'Til you find yourself lookin'
Across Farewell Bend

Now the Oregon country
Unfolds like a dream
And a Garden of Eden
We're told it will be
'Til we reached the Blue Mountains
And it started to snow
And some didn't make it
Past there to the coast

The Columbia takes you
When you're down on your knees
It rushes and pushes you
Home to the sea
And the Willamette Valley
Is a paradise
To those who survived
This perilous flight

I'll tell my story
Of the Oregon Trail
And hope my account of the truth
Shall be fair
I'd lost all faith
In what to believe
'Til I found my own words
To say what I'd seen

We crossed the great plains
And the great divide
And the wilderness country
On the other side
If I'd known of the hardships
Before we began
I'd have taken a ship
To the Oregon sand

Oh the journey through life
Is the destiny
For all women and men
All colors and creed
We ache for the comforts
Of body and soul
Like the pilgrims who travelled
This Oregon road

2000 miles
And six months of road
If you don't leave in May
You'll die in the snow
Oh the many who travelled
And the many who fell
Gambled all they had
On the Oregon Trail ♪

Canadian River ♪

There's a river down in Texas
In the north part of the state
And they say there's many a story
Of how it came to have it's name
Well it's a ragged old kind of river
It runs shallow and it runs wide
But when you're dyin' for a drink son
You know the water tastes like wine

I came down from the northland
On the great northern plains
Joined an outfit on the Pecos
Somewhere south of Santa Fe
From the Goodnight and the Loving
To the old Chisholm Trail
I did a lot of cowboyin'
Before the comin' of the rails

We rode up the Panhandle
On a northern cattle drive
We'd be crossing Oklahoma
On the trail to Illinois
We made camp down by this river
And across the southern sky
The lights of Amarillo
Drew me back for one more night

I was ridin' on the night herd
With another buckaroo
I said I'd give him a silver dollar

If he wouldn't say a word
And under cover of the darkness
I quietly slipped away
Back to Amarillo
And the girl who waited there

Now the lights of Amarillo
Lead many men astray
But the gal that I was courtin'
Knew I'd marry her some day
And the mornin' came too early
When I heard the awful sounds
Gunfire and thunder
From the river north of town

I rode back to the cow camp
To see what had been done
Commanches struck at daybreak
And they killed near everyone
The herd was all stampeded
And there'd soon be hell to pay
If the bossman back in Austin
Ever knew where I had been

No time to tell my darlin'
I'm leavin' here today
I'll go back home to Canada
If I can make my getaway
I'll follow this old river
Across Oklahoma to St. Lou
Take a steamer up the river
And then I'll send for you

Canadian River
You're a long way from home
Don't you ever get weary
Of always movin' on
But if I could go with you
I wouldn't feel so all alone
Canadian River
Won't you carry me home

Yes I came down from the northland
On the great northern plains
Joined an outfit on the Pecos
Somewhere south of Santa Fe
From the Goodnight and the Loving
To the old Chisholm Trail
I think I've finally seen the end
Of my wilder cowboy days

There's a river down in Texas
In the north part of the state
And I lived to tell my story
Of how it all came down on me
Well it's a ragged old kind of river
It runs shallow and it runs wide
But when you're dyin' for a drink son
You know the water tastes like wine

Canadian River
You're a long way from home
Don't you ever get weary
Of always movin' on
But if I could go with you
I wouldn't feel so all alone
Canadian River
Won't you carry me home ♪

Cattle Drive ♪

I am a workin' cowboy
I live out on the range
This is the life I've chosen
I'm never gonna' change
Just like the mustang that I ride
The wild heart still remains
And there's something in a cowboy
That never will be tamed

I've heard them tales from long ago
When first the white man came
When Spanish horse and cattle
Scattered wild across the plains
The rangeland was wide open
And the west was wild and new
And the first wild broncs were broken
By the Indian buckaroo

From the Yellowhead to the Yellowstone
Across the Great Divide
From the Rio Grande to the Caribou
This is where the cowboys ride
More than a hundred years of history
Underneath this great big sky
Well the damdest thing we ever did
Was to work on a cattle drive

I never was the kind to like
This gettin' up for dawn
Especially when it's rainin'
And I'm frozen like the ground
But I start feelin' better boys
When I smell that coffee on
And ol' cookie's slingin' bacon
And singin' a cattle song

I like to sing a gentle song
To keep myself awake
While ridin' on the night herd
For to keep them cattle safe
I dream about my sweetheart
And I sing a lonesome tune
'Cuz it's me and a bunch of coyotes
In a choir beneath the moon

From the Thompson and Chilcotin
Over New Caledonia way
And from Texas west to Oregon
And the great northern plains
The great trail herds were driven
Through the wind and snow and rain
By the damdest bunch you ever saw
The cowboys on the open range

Goodbye my darlin'
I'll see you next year
If I ever survive
This cattle drive ♪

Longhorns

I write about the northern range
And the northern mysteries
And I dream about the sunny slopes
That I have yet to see

I'll find a southern range someday
Like where the longhorns first began
It may take some time until I find
My trail of golden sand

Far across the wild Atlantic
And along the Spanish Main
The longhorns began their journey
From those Andalusian plains

And like Vikings who once set sail
To find these New World shores
With longhorns did they greet their foe
And quaff their mead and ale

And I may grow my whiskers long
And even wear longhorns myself someday
Until I reach my own Rio Grande
And a Goodnight-Loving's Trail

For we are here but a short time
And may do just as we please
To climb our chosen mountain
And find our own heart's dream

Like the Vikings and the longhorns
And all of us who hope
Someday to find our own Valhalla
On a sunny southern slope

They Rode The Plains ♪

They rode the plains
Each and every one
They followed their dreams
And they followed the sun
And though some be forgotten
The legends remain
Of a spirit unbroken
When they rode the plains

First came the red man
On the western plains
He captured Spanish horses
Running wild on the range
But for the first real Americans
The day would surely come
These proud and mighty nations
Would see the setting of the sun

Then came the white man
Like a blizzard to the plains
He would change the landscape
But keep the Indian names
And as the buffalo vanished
And the cattle herds grew
And the old west gave way
To the changes comin' through

And there were many others
And they rode the plains
The Mexican vaqueros
And the wild mountain men
The rebels and the ranchers
And the runaway slaves
And the women who loved them
And the women who stayed

And of all the ones who rode the plains
What some would lose and others gain
The legends of the west remain
In our poetry and song
And though time and circumstance may change
The passion for the open range
Still burns out here like a fiery flame
In a land still free and strong

And they ride the plains
Each and every one
They follow their dreams
And they follow the sun
And though some be forgotten
The legends remain
Of a spirit unbroken
When they ride the plains ♪

Silver Gate

Deep in the heart of the Yellowstone
South of the old Bozeman Trail
Way back in the Absarokas
Is a place I remember so well

We headed out west in the summertime
Me and my sister Louise
We were hoping to find a better life
At the end of the Oregon Trail

By the time we got to Cheyenne
The weather turned bitterly cold
So we accepted an offer of employment
Up north at Bill Cody's hotel

The brand new Irma Hotel, we were told
Was a fine establishment indeed
We could make good money as hostesses
And then leave for the coast in the spring

So we travelled by stage up to Sheridan
And west through the Bighorn Range
'Til we rolled into Cody Wyoming
Where we had expected to stay

The Irma Hotel was a beauty indeed
A palace for the pleasures of men
And the cherrywood bar and the chandeliers
Were like nothing that we'd ever seen

But such was not our good fortune
To remain in such lavish repair
For we were soon bundled off further northward
To the camptown of Silver Gate there

And deep in the Absarokas
Me and my sister Louise
Became the ladies of gentlemen's pleasure
In Silver Gate and all who came there

We were two young gals from Ohio
We had come west to start a new life
But we found ourselves taken advantage
By men who had other designs

That winter was long and so bitter
And the second was more of the same
My hopes lay like tarnished old silver
In the hills 'round Silver Gate there

Well we scrimped and we saved and we toiled
We laughed and we cried and I prayed
Some day that I would be delivered
From Silver Gate and all my despair

I escaped from Silver Gate Montana
And I made it across to the coast
To my golden gate dreams of San Francisco
Where I finally have realized my hopes

Louise stayed on in Montana
And met a man of equal ambition
And together they built and did manage
A new house of pleasure out there

I never returned to Montana
Or saw Louise ever again
Though she stayed in that hotel business
And made for herself quite a name

So if you're ever in southern Montana
Down on the Yellowstone trail
You can still spend the night at Louise's hotel
In the camptown of old Silver Gate

Golden Years ♪

I remember the day
When he passed away
And I stood by the side of his grave
When the words
I used to hear him say
Came to me in this song that I sing

Sure hope the next forty
Ain't like the back forty
As I look back through the years
Sure hope the next forty
Ain't like the back forty
As I sew my golden years

Well he worked the land
And he took a stand
Seven children they raised on the way
When he took him a wife
And they lived a fine life
And they loved 'til his dying day

There was sorrow and pain
There was shortage of rain
And they never broke even those years
Times were hungry and lean
And though he never got mean
Some days he couldn't hold back the tears

There were seasons of pain
When the tears fell like rain
When it seemed there was nothing to gain
All the winters of snow
And the forty below
He always said that you reap what you sew
Yes he believed
That you reap what you sew

Now I look at my life
All the trouble and strife
And I wonder how the future will be
Will I take me a wife
Will we build a fine life
And love through our golden years

I remember the day
When he passed away
And I stood by the side of his grave
When the words
I used to hear him say
Came to me in this song that I sing

Sure hope the next forty
Ain't like the back forty
As I look back through the years
Sure hope the next forty
Ain't like the back forty
As I sew my golden years ♪

Dustbowl Diary

1929 –
Grasses begin shrivelling
Trees bending, withering
Sloughs drying up
Livestock begin starving
People crying
Prairie suffocating
Nothing growing
To fruition
Only dissipating
Remains
Of what was stored
From better harvests until
The old begin dying, though
Some hang on because
They had given everything
To come here
In hope –

And the very young
Dying, or surviving
As their mothers do
Looking for hope
Anywhere
And leaving or staying
Above or below
This parched ground
Where all are grieving

Heaving
As Black Blizzard topsoils
Blow from here to Ontario
Leaving overploughed fields
And a barren decade
Finally baked and cracked
Like an empty piecrust
Through the heat waves
Of '36 and '37 –

The Dustbowl
Took few prisoners
But left many
Learning the hard lessons
Whether they stayed
Or moved on
As did my father –
When he left
In search of
A new kind of harvest

Below The Border ♪

I met her in a small town
Just below the border
Raven hair in ringlets
Fell down upon her shoulders
I know that I can't stay
But how I hate to go
What more can I say
In the hope that she will wait

The journeys of a lifetime
Can sometimes leave you colder
But love is more than passion
When you're feeling older
And I was on the run
From the memories of the past
All the things I'd left undone
And a love that didn't last

Yes I was on the run
Accused of things I hadn't done
But I swore no lawman's gun
Would ever bring me down

So I left her in that small town
Just below the border
South of Ensenada
In Baja California
She said that she would pray
And wait for my return
If I can only clear my name
And live to hold her once again ♪

Cowboys, Cowgirls, 'n Poets

"….Perhaps that's why in self defense
I became a poet…"

Cow Poetry

Cow poetry
Is no mere flakey flurry
Of non-sequiturs
Loose words, puns and errant slurs

Cow poetry
Is no mere slip of the tongue
No slippery cow slick
Or simple tongue in cheek gone wrong

Cow poetry starts
When you fall in love
With every natural thing
Under western sun and stars

And then when a thought or mood
Takes you by surprise
Like watchin' a hawk
Dive right out of the sky

You rush to write it down
On anything, as fast as you can
Before it's come and gone
Like every setting sun

Then it's about choosing your words
With the utmost of care
In the hope that a poem
Soon will be there

For finding the perfect word
Brings an exhilaration
Like ropin' a fine young stallion
From a wild stampedin' herd

And it doesn't matter much
Where you've come from
Or how many bulls you've rode
Or buckles you say you've won

'Cuz when you first write down
Your very own cow poem
Or simple country song
You know you believe, you know you belong

So you see my friend
Cow poetry is no mere triviality
For just like Homer's Odyssey
It's part of our Western history

And we would be remiss
If we failed to honour the Cow
With whose name we take such liberties
As she's been so very patient with us,
outstanding in her field

The Finals In Cheyenne ♪

She thought she'd go to Denver
Start all over if she can
So she called him from a payphone
And she lied to him again

She said I'm bound for California
Maybe live out on the coast
Don't you bother tryin' to follow
You can't hold what you've lost

We're just different kinds of people
Chasin' different kinds of dreams
You make a livin' tryin' to hold on
I just wanted to be free

So put your mind back on the horses
And I'll make other plans
Anyway I wish you good luck
At the finals in Cheyenne

She got tired of travellin' with him
Down his rodeo road
And all the broken promises
And the lies that they told

Like he's gonna' quit the circuit
If she'd give him one more chance
To finally win the big one
At the finals in Cheyenne

They're just different kinds of people
Chasin' different kinds of dreams
He makes a livin' tryin' to hold on
She just wanted to be free

He'll put his mind back on the horses
She'll probably find another man
And there's different kinds of losin'
At the finals in Cheyenne

Two different kinds of losin'
At the finals in Cheyenne ♪

Cowboys, Coffins 'n Cadillacs ♪

Cowboys 'n coffins 'n cadillacs
When they all ride together
There'll be no turnin' back
Put a cowboy in a coffin in a Cadillac
Take him up yonder
To the heavenly shack

C is for cowboys
Long may they ride
'Cross the wide Missouri
And the Great Divide
Tall in the saddle he's a free man when he rides
He'll ride forever like the clouds in the sky

C is for coffins
And the whisperin' pines
When the cold wind whistles
You can hear them cry
When you lay down your burdens,
at the end of the line
Your coffin will carry you to the last goodbye

C it a – comin'
It's a Cadillac
Swing low sweet chariot
So long and black
Carry this cowboy on his final ride
Carry him up yonder to his home in the sky

Long may they ride
Long may they ride
From the prairies to the foothills
And the valleys deep and wide
I sure hope they don't all say
Goodbye ♪

Cowboy Heaven

My home is on the open range
Under this great big sky
Over the plains and foothills
And along the Great Divide
Out here on the western range
It's really no mystery
My home is out here all right
It's cowboy heaven to me

Now people dream of heaven
As if it's some place far away
They work and pray and do their best
Hopin' they'll get there some fine day
But a cowboy knows about heaven
He works there every day
He knows his place is on the land
Livin' the cowboy way

So this is it right here and now
As good as its gonna' get
It's all in the attitude
And what you make of it
It's always in the simple things
That heaven can be found
Just look out across the range
And listen to the sound

Horses And Hills ♪

The cattle are quiet, the horses are still
Sun goin' down, over yonder hill
It's been a long day, and we've done our best
Me and my pony, we're goin' home to rest

I lead my pony, back to the barn
Throw my chaps and reins, up on the wall
A little water and hay, and a good cigar
And the time to think on, how lucky we are

Down in the valley, up along the ridge
We ride together, like a couple of kids
No part of the West, that we ain't seen
'Cuz me and my pony, we're livin' our dreams

I'll follow these trails
Wherever they take me
'Long as there's still, horses and hills
I'll follow my dreams
Wherever they lead me
'Long as I can ride, horses and hills

These horses and hills

Horses and hills

Horses

and

Hills ♪

Ivan Daines' Rodeo Picknic

Way out west of Innisfail
Up along Alberta's Cowboy Trail
You'll find a good time without fail
At Ivan Daines' Rodeo Picknic

Now every year about the end of July
When the summer sun is ridin' high
People gather here from far and wide
At the Daines' family ranch

Now it might rain, hail or snow
Tornado winds might whip and blow
But stuff like that never keeps us away
From the Daines' long weekend rodeo

For we rodeo by day
And party all night long
Live music gets goin' by noon
And goes on pretty much 'til dawn

There's burgers and beer
Knockwurst and pretzels
So you can eat your fill
And wet your whistle

There's a big bonfire
Every single night
Where folks meet and mingle
And even get a little tight

Come Sunday mornin' it's time for worship
Pancakes 'n eggs and maple syrup
Gospel, bluegrass and time for reflection
Good neighbours livin' in respect and affection

Nobody ever gets too outta' line
Or causes a ruckus or such waste of time
'Cuz it's a family affair for young and old
And the focus is on what's good for the soul

Everything goes down
Just as smoothe as apple pie
Under Ivan Daines'
Watchful rodeo pro's eye

Good natured by nature
Mature and always fair
The man's a true cowboy
With talent to spare

So if you've got a yen
To find a real good time
You won't go wrong
North of ol' 49

Just keep on goin'
Past what they call Gasoline Alley
'Til you're smack dab in the middle
Of Alberta's Tornado Valley

Turn west on the gravel for a few dusty miles
Then you'll soon be very pleasantly surprised
To find a whole lot of good ol' frolic and fun
On a ranch as pretty as the mornin' sun

The weekend's packed with acres of fun
From Thursday 'til Monday and sun-up 'til dawn
There's plenty of music and rodeo action
It's a guaranteed tank full of real satisfaction

Come Monday it's time to take 'er all down
Pack up your gear and head down the line
Another year's party has come and gone
And it's time to shake hands and say so long

For movin' on can bring a tear to your eye
Like watchin' Lonesome Dove every single time
But the wheel turns 'round,
so you don't have to fear
There'll be another rodeo picknic right here,
next year!

Prairie Rose ♪

She's goin' to the prairies
She's goin' to the sun
She likes the way those northern lights
Shine down on Edmonton
She's pullin' up the old roots
And she's gonna' plant the new
She's goin' to the prairies
Gonna' make her dreams come true

She's tired of the nightlife
She's tired of the pain
She's tired of the grey skies
And six long months of rain
She's packin' up the old ways
And she's gonna' start anew
She's goin' to the prairies
Gonna' make her dreams come true

And the wild prairie rose
Is still her favourite flower
Even though she's been away so long
She's not forgotten how
All the riches in the world
Don't make a house a home
She's a wild prairie rose
And she's on her way back home ♪

Old Fashioned New Age Cowboy ♪

I'm just an old fashioned new age cowboy
When I say hi that means howdy
Now put me on a plane, or home on the range
Either way I'm okay, except on Mondays

I'm just a new fangled good ol' kind o' boy
And I like them new age kind of toys
No matter where I roam, I never feel alone
'Cuz I always pack my laptop and my
cellular phone

Yippi-yi-o-ky-yay,
today's another brand new day
For this old fashioned new age cowboy

I want an old fashioned new age romance
With a gal who'll teach me how to dance
Deep in the south of France,
we'll find ourselves a ranch
And when we miss the snow,
why we'll just wing our way back home

I like most everything country style
And I like to walk a country mile
Got an old pair of cowboy boots,
for to ride rope and shoot
But the rest of the time, sandals suit me fine

Yippi--yi-o-ky-yay,
today's another brand new day
For this old fashioned new age cowboy

Well this ol' world keeps on changin' day to day
So it helps to laugh along the way
When you feel yourself gettin' old,
try to lighten up that load
And when you work or play,
why you'll just sing those blues away

So yippi-yi-o-ky-yay,
today's another brand new day
For this old fashioned new age cowboy
I'm just an old fashioned new age
New age
Cowboy ♪

For Casey

She is such a winsome lass
that's plain enough to see
And I am just an old train wreck
how could it ever be
But oh how her golden hair
and wistful western smile
Can lead an old freight train like me
to dream just once in a while

Now she could wear a string of pearls
or a pair of old blue jeans
It wouldn't change a thing about
how she looks to me
For she is like the graceful swan
gliding gently down the stream
Her eyes are like the diamond sands
in every cowboy's dream

I never intended to feel this way
or take to poetry
Like William Blake who came to know
that fearful symmetry
The feeling poets only feel
when finding natural beauty
Which they may have only seen before
in dream and fantasy

I'd like to sing with her some day
if there ever was a way
Or even walk a mile with her
along this life's highway
But I am just a poet
who was ever meant to dream
And we are like the passing trains
across the wide prairie

Nevertheless I must confess
I'd sing with her someday
To hear that kind of harmony
I'd ride near anywhere
For the cowboy life is lonesome
and a poet's even more
And to sing of love and longing
is what a poet's for

What to say and what to do
how to put it into words
These questions cut the poet out
from the many passing herds
And keep us up too late at night
waiting for sunrise
The cowboy poet dreams of love
within a woman's eyes

I'll go back to the ranching
I'll go back to the range
Back to what I know the best
though it seems that I have changed
For once you've seen such beauty
how do you soon forget
Perhaps that's why in self defense
I became a poet

Yes she is such a winsome lass
that's plain enough to see
And I am but a poet
out on the lone prairie
But oh how her golden voice
and wistful western smile
Can lead an old cowboy like me
to dream just once in a while

And every time I hear her sing
that's when I hear the music
The bells of heaven seem so near
whenever Casey sings

The Cowboy In Me ♪

Day after day, I drive into town
Sometimes I don't get back home again
until the evenin' sun goes down
And day after day, I work for my pay
I'll be the first in line
when somebody finds a better way

Day after day, there's always somethin' new
Just when you think you've done it all
there's always one more thing to do
And when you work for somebody else
don't you find it true
Nine times out of ten
you've got to compromise your point of view

But when the workin' day is through
I know just what to do
to unwind
I've got a piece of paradise
And with my lover by my side
I'll feel fine

I'm gonna' ride, over the plains
I'm gonna' ride above the clouds and the rain
And I can soar like an eagle
in my dreams
Just as free as I can be
that's the cowboy in me

Oh don't you wanna' go
Oh don't you wanna' go with me

We're gonna' ride, over the plains
we're gonna' ride above the clouds and the rain
And we can soar like eagles
in our dreams
Just as free as we can be
that's the cowboy in me ♪

Lonesome Cowgirl ♪

You're walkin' away little darlin'
You say you're sorry that we'll be apart
But remember when you're on the road my darlin'
You'll be walkin' away with my heart

You said to me, you need to see the world
The world of diamonds rubies and pearls
But do you know the love you'll be leavin'
Is more precious than all those other jewels

"Now I'm a wiser lonesome cowgirl
I had to leave a dream or two behind
But the lessons I'm learning on this journey
Are more precious than the diamonds in a mine"

Well I read that lonesome cowgirl's letter
With a grateful teardrop in my eye
She's following her very own heart's roadmap
Out under that endless western sky

Perhaps we'll meet again up yonder
Or when we cross the Great Divide
Perhaps we'll even find a season
To walk again together side by side

We all belong to Mother Nature
In faith and hope and honesty
Just play the cards before you fold them
And the sun and the moon are for free ♪

A Post-Modern Cowboy Lament ♪

Ridin' the range of emotion
Swingin' from my family tree
Sometimes I get the notion
It's high time I tried therapy

Tossed like a ship on the ocean
Driftin' along with the tide
Sometimes a wave of emotion
Shipwreck's my ego inside

As a young boy I felt some frustration
In my family constellation
It was hard to find my place,
but I came through with grace
Judgin' by my reputation

Now I could tell you some stories
About childhood and survival
I'm an adult child and I like to get wild
Singin' my songs and stories

And I tip my hat to my uncle
He's only seventy-five
And his young bride to be, she's seventy-three
It's sure good to see young love alive

And I've learned to trust in my senses
My mind is happy and free
When I live in present tenses,
I don't need defenses
And the future looks better to me

So throw me a rodeo rope
And pull me safely to shore
Please don't let go-e-o
I need your love to survive ♪

This Side Of The Rockies ♪

Don't like the rain, day after day
Livin' in the pourin' rain
Only interrupts my game
Sign of the times, dark clouds up above
Half a year and more in the pourin' rain
Ain't what I'm dreamin' of

Don't like the smog, or livin' in a permanent fog
Big smokin' city air
I wouldn't want to feed my dog
Sign of the times, smokestacks up above
On the one hand there's a nuclear reactor
On the other hand a garbage dump

Oh Canada, better think while you still can
Do you wanna' sell your soul
To your big old Uncle Sam
Don't drink the water, better not eat the fish
Livin' in a concrete jungle
Never was my sacred wish

But this side of the Rockies
This side of the line
This side of the Rockies
Gonna' shine, gonna' shine

This side of the Rockies
The sun most always shines
Still room enough
To just cut loose and ride
Ride, ride
Ride

This side of the Rockies
This side of the line
This side of the Rockies
Gonna' shine, gonna' shine ♪

The Cowboy Hat

Now the cowboy hat
is a fine invention
When I put one on
I attract more attention
And when I wear my hat
when I go to the city
People look at me as if
I'm some exotic species

When you wear The Hat
it don't matter what kind
You walk with a swagger
and you ain't quite so shy
These days I prefer
the Tom Mix style
It adds a foot to my height
but it feels like a mile

You get way more for your money
than with a baseball cap
You get a peak that runs clear 'round
the whole dang hat
Now I can appreciate the Green Berets
the Mounties and ol' Davie Crockett
But when it came to their headgear
why they just plum lost it

In the good ol' days of rodeo
yer hat took quite a beatin'
'Cuz when you got bucked off
why yer hat would go a-flyin'
But these days some folks keep their hats
dry and nice and perty
They even cover 'em up in plastic
so they never get wet or dirty

But if you're a workin' cowboy
and you can afford it
You've got a workin' hat by day
and a fancy Dan to party
And if you're a western devotee
or a challenged cow poet like me
Why you may wear a bunch of hats
hell maybe even two or three

You'll proudly line 'em up
on your top floor bedroom shelf
Or hang 'em on an antler rack
down in your big front hall
They'll hang there in their majesty
for all the world to see
They symbolize your passion
for western chivalry

The cowboy hat means many things
to cowpeople short and tall
We wear it through the best and worst
and whether big or small
The feature of the cowboy hat
that's prized most of all
Is the secret it will faithfully conceal
when you know you're goin' bald

Western Wind ♪

It's the western wind
that brings me home to you
When the work's all done
and the season's through
When I've had my fill
of this rodeo trail
And I've lost the will
for anything but you
And the western wind

It's the full moon light
and the stars above
That drew me close to you
so we could fall in love
Under the western sky
back when we were young
When the days grew short
because our nights were long
In the western wind

It's the way you smile
and the way we touch
The fire in your eyes
that always says so much
About the way we've loved
since the day we met
When we were swept away
with no regret
By the western wind

And the western wind
turned my life around
Just like a breath of spring
upon the frozen ground
And the western wind
still takes my breath away
Just like the big Chinook
on a winter's day
It's the western wind ♪

Outlaws, Heroes 'n Such

"….Tell me have you heard in Texas
When the sun goes down tonight
There'll be another crime in Texas
This time they could have spared the life…"

Charlie And Bill

Charlie and Bill
Met in central Montana
Somewhere in the 1890's
In the heat and the dust
Near the end of the open range
And they shared something unusual in common
In how they responded to all they had seen

When they first came to Montana
They were both pretty green
Each one of them no more than the age of 16
They had come for the adventure
Of the real cowboy life
Though what they would thence come to be
Neither one could have foreseen

For they had come at that singular time
On the cusp of plains history
When cattle replaced the bison
Inside of thirty-odd short years
When the whole West was changing
Before everybody's eyes…but
Charlie and Bill were of the few,
with special insight

Now of the two, Charlie Russell came first
Back in 1880 out of old St. Lou
At the age of 16 then what else would you do
But hire on as a wrangler
In hopes of adventure and survival
Though Charlie soon saw much more
Of what he would do with the rest of his life

17 years the younger, Bill Sinclair arrived
And in 1897 rode on his first cattle drive
From Orin Junction north to old Fort Benton
He'd been on the run out of Saskatchewan
A Scot given much to thought
He reflected on what he saw
And soon had an inkling to write it all down

The first cattle came north before they arrived
Brought up from Texas in the early 60's
The DHS moved onto Judith Basin in '79
And Bill worked for the TL and Circle Diamond
But by that time Charlie had settled down
There were fences, stockyards and bigger towns
'Til by 1900 there were more sheep than cattle,
on the ancient buffalo ground

They had come for the adventure
And they had come to live the life
They had the stars in their eyes
And the myths in their minds
They had come to be cowboys
And in following their dreams
They transformed into art all they did see

Charlie became the painter
And in his wild early years
He sketched and he painted
And he lived as he pleased
Until a fine young woman
Helped transform the boy to the man
Who could show the true colors of the West,
to the rest of the world

And Bill was more the wrangler
Determined to ride forever
Until through barbed wire fences
He saw the bull written on the wall
And it occurred to his keen sense of justice
That the world ought to know
The story of the real cowboy way of life

They would meet again later, in 1904
And often at the new Mint Saloon
In downtown Great Falls, where
Charlie's paintings came to hang on the wall
And Bill began to live and write there full time
Both were so captivated by the awe they felt
In the long silent hours devoted to their art

Charlie painted his vision
For the rest of his life
And comforted and guided
By his faithful young wife
Forever the dreamer
He lived for what he'd seen
The Golden West, and the real cowboy dream

Bill moved back to Canada
And re-invented himself once again
A rugged survivor
He would never quite come to rest
But he came to love the sea
And as he followed the salmon
He still found a way to feel wild and free

And being true artists, they knew it was over
Before it had ended
The wide open spaces
Without borders or fences
And they knew like the Redman
What it meant to live a free life
In a time when the West was a paradise

Charlie and Bill
They saw the real deal
And always stayed true to their cowboy ideals
They set an example for the rest of us to follow
As we write our poems, paint our pictures
Braid our rope and sing our songs
In keepin' the flame of the real West alive

Kootenai Brown

I can't quite recall
when I first heard your name
Kootenai Brown –
but earlier this year
I picked up a book in Banff
attracted as I was
by your name
the buckskin that you wore
and that distant look in your eye

And when I scanned the cover and learned
that none less than Grant MacEwan –
a hero himself to many an eye
regarded you as a true Canadian hero
well I was hooked and ready

to read between the lines
about how you got your name
the buckskin that you wore
and that distant look in your eye

I read that book from cover to cover
a decent effort by an admiring author –
and being myself of British Isles descent
I can understand something of what lead you
to leave the old world behind
and live your life in the Golden West
falling in love with what you found
the Shining Mountains, the Great Plains
and the ancient Buffalo Ground

Born on the Emerald Isle
and through your grandmother's tireless toil
you went on to serve in India
'til round the Cape of Good Hope
you dreamed a dream of freedom
and with your friend
young Arthur Vowell
you landed in America
on the northwest Pacific coast –
you searched for gold and wealth
like conquistadors of old
but your respect for life was not driven
by some singular belief or greed
and so you dared not take a life
without the direst of need

A reasonable man
with an open heart
you soon found yourself
in the thick of it
where it was all too often

kill or be killed –
do all you can
and then left to wonder
what does it mean to be the last to survive?

And when you crossed the Rockies
and rode for the pony express
you saw the buffalo thick as locust
and out there in the tall grass
you said you were captured by Sitting Bull
the father of the Sioux –
now did you escape
or did he let you slip away
as if by some decree of destiny at play?

Kootenai Brown –
I've been through the land
where you settled down
by the Waterton Lakes
along the eastern slope
the breathtaking world
of what people once called
the Shining Mountains
and Going To The Sun

And sometimes I think I can't live anymore
in a modern world
so far from people like you
and Sitting Bull –
this world of plastic, plastic and more
where the blood of the buffalo is forgotten
and cities where 9 out of 10 have no idea
that.these were once sacred places –
as they are still
or where most of these place names
originally came from –

no, you never said a lot in words
Kootenai Brown
but I bet you'd understand tonight
something of where I'm coming from

Karla Faye ♪

Tell me have they heard of Jesus
Do they worship in his name
And if the message is compassion
How can they kill again
Tell me have you heard in Texas
When the sun goes down tonight
There'll be another crime in Texas
This time they could have spared the life

Karla Faye was given heroin
when she was only ten
She was sent out on the street
to sell herself to men
And like Mary Magdalena
she found Jesus as a friend
After two thousand years
haven't men learned anything?

Karla Faye grew up in prison
like so many young ones do
She became a model prisoner
just as kind as me and you
And in 14 years on death row
in a crazy kind of way
It was the first time in her young life
that she had ever felt safe

She died on a wednesday evening
I was watching CNN
Executed down in Texas
from Waco on to Heaven
And the world watched and waited
for the governor to decide
He was playin' it cool 'til the very end
but he would not change his mind

In the land we call America
where they say they're number one
Where it's hard to get some health care
but it's easier to buy a gun
And if one eye costs another
how can two eyes learn to see
And if one crime deserves another
how can wounds ever heal

Tell me have they heard of Jesus
Do they worship in his name
And if the message is forgiveness
How can they kill again
Tell me have you heard in Texas
When the sun goes down tonight
There'll be another crime in Texas
This time they could have spared the life ♪

Black Diamond Saloon ♪

Way out in the foothills
where the sunshine never ends
Down in southern Alberta
where your neighbour is your friend
Another week of workin'
just about drove me around the bend
So I jump in my truck and I head for town
and another wild weekend

Now Lennette she sings so pretty
Edna's behind the bar
Tommy plays the spoons real good
and I strum my old guitar
And Peter plays the slide you know
we like it when he sings the blues
On another Saturday afternoon
at the old Black Diamond Saloon

So you made it to the weekend
and you're lookin' for something to do
Come on down and paint the town
at the old Black Diamond Saloon
Put some gas in the car and bring your guitar
and maybe even pick a tune
On another Saturday afternoon
at the old Black Diamond Saloon

Another Saturday afternoon
at the old Black Diamond Saloon
Don't worry about tomorrow
tonight we're gonna' hang the moon
Well we may all go straight to hell
but now we're makin' time stand still
On another Saturday afternoon
at the old Black Diamond Saloon ♪

In The Stillness Of The Wilderness

For a moment
Just a moment
There... in the cabin
The two of us
And outside our window
A mottled mountain sky
Trees unmoved
In blissful peace
When suddenly
The loud retort
Of cannon fire
In the quiet of the cabin
The stillness shattered
I swear
By the fart of my partner
A sudden blast which
Shocked the crows
Into frenzied flight
And caused the trees
To quiver in fright
And in our avalanche of laughter
The mountain of stillness
Did crumble

My Old Tent

I was planning to head out once again
On a late summer expedition
And I somehow sensed the need
For a sturdy new rendition
Perhaps to retire the old veteran
And make this a year of transition

I had thought why even bring her along
Her poles are mostly splintered
And there's tears in her walls
But since she has followed me well
Like a faithful old pack mule
I just hate to put her down
Oh what the hell, let's bring her along

So I pitched my old tent
Next to the one which was new
And as I looked at them both
Like a real estate tycoon
From my reclining camp chair
I thought well –
It's good to see my old friend risen once again

Like an old prize fighter
Who's fought too many a round
And absorbed many heavy blows for me
How fond I feel of her now
As she stands there in her tattered colours
So proudly once again
In the early evening western sun

I gaze at her faded nylon walls
The violet and green long blanched by the sun
Her poles reinforced by duck tape and twine
The price she has paid to come along for the ride
And soon I'm reflecting as best as I can
On how our adventures first had begun

Like two young comrades
Joining the French Foreign Legion
We ran away together
For the sheer joy of boyish adventure
And the urge for going became our theme song
And even though she never said much
She was there all along

From the Great Lake shores
And those reckless autumn winds
Lashing tree branches and leaves
Against her sturdy willing walls
She braced with determination
And she sheltered me well
Through the thick and the thin of Ontario's fall

And across the broad plains
We have camped and wandered
Up through Qu'Appelle Valley
Down into the Cypress Hills
We've shared story and song
With many a fellow traveller
And as many a beer as the stories were long

Then into the foothills
And on to the mountains
We nested like migratory birds
By rivers and natural fountains
And drawn like bees to the nectar
Of nature's sweet cathedral gardens
In Rocky Mountain meadows and spires

And over the mountains
And on to the coast
Deep into the evergreens
And west of the west
The enchanted trails of the Pacific Crest
Until by soft ocean tidal pools
We have come at last to take some rest

We've followed these trails
Like pilgrims on our chosen path
We've shared music and words
At gatherings and festivals
And then sought the quieter places
For which the soul longs
As Mother Nature's grateful guests

We've weathered her thunder
And seen Nature's ire
The big hailstorms in august
And Tornado Alley fire
The 24 hour straight downpours
We somehow survived –
In the end of it all we just both gave a sigh

Beneath my old friend's sheltering dome
I've listened to the wind
And written poem and song
We've followed my dreams
From sunset to sunrise
And turned with the earth
As she's turned with the sun

And as I watch the smoke curl
Through the campfire tonight
My old friend stands patiently
Silently nearby
Memories rise up and drift with the wind
Back to my boyhood –
The first thrill of camping

At camp I've found in my imagination
A link with the past and glorious traditions
Of Crudaser knights and Mongol hordes
The jungles of Arica and Aztec gold
From the Iroquois forest to Custer's last stand
For all of us who camp and live close to the land
It's camping transforms the boy to a man

And now as I write late
And slowly into twilight
The sky changing colours
Over great western red cedars
My old friend stands waiting
To give her best once again
As I write that together yet –
We're two indeed, who have seen the west

Robbery In Black Diamond ♪

In the town of Black Diamond
not so long ago
In the summer of '97
a story did unfold
The heat of a summer's evening
still hung in the midnight air
When the riders descended
on the hotel there

Well the bar was half empty
on the tail of a long weekend
And no one there suspected
that life would soon depend
On the mood of a bunch of outlaws
and what they did intend
They were carryin' sawed off shotguns
and they didn't give a damn

Just give us your silver
and give us your gold
Get down on your knees
and do what you're told
We just want your money
so you must decide
If you want to give us trouble
it'll be your day to die

Well a few short days later
up north in Calgary
Did the same ones strike again
did they carry on that spree
Wearin' the mask of a clown
so you couldn't really tell
Would they be the same ones
robbed the old Black Diamond Hotel

In the town of Black Diamond
just like days of old
Well they robbed the old Black Diamond
5000 I'm told
A poor man's desperation
made him steal from his own kind
Now was it just a bad seed
or the temper of the times

And where are they now
where are they now
They probably crossed the border
Montana by now
And where will it be
in one too many a town
When the guns of law and order
finally bring them fellas down ♪

Son Gone Wrong ♪

The year was 1989
when he broke out of jail
Now the whole damn country
has set out on his trail
He climbed a fence, cut his hands
and tore himself free
Jed Merrell
what makes you think you'll ever get away

Now this is not the first time
that he broke out of jail
He spent damn near half his life
inside them prison cells
Prison taught him how to be
a master criminal
Now he's on the loose
he'll make 'em pay and raise some hell

Now which side of the law
is your mama really on
She had to raise you up herself
when your daddy moved along
She once slipped you a gun in jail
to help you escape
But in her heart she knows
she helps to keep you the same

Some say it's the devil
that makes a man this way
Throw money at the problem
and hope it goes away

But the way things are goin'
in this country today
Someday near half the country
just might be locked away

And what is it that makes a man
treat women this way
What makes him turn against them
and stalk them like prey
Driven by some need
for love or revenge
I hope some day he sees
it's his choice how it ends

Now this is not a song
to praise the man or what he's done
And a mother's love was not enough
to save a son gone wrong
But soon he'll get hungry
and he'll try to strike again
And if he isn't taken down
he'll only cause more pain

Son gone wrong
a man without a heart
It makes you wonder
how things ever start
A modern day outlaw
could be any other name
Jed Merrell
what makes you think you'll ever get away ♪

The Ballad Of Brooks & Jones ♪

I was drinkin' one night in a tavern
I was listenin' to the sweet country sound
Just a man with his guitar,
sang his songs for the bar
And I was happy just holdin' my own

When a fool sat down beside me
He was already three sheets to the wind
I could tell he was the kind,
who just had to speak his mind
Even though he hardly had one left to own

He said mister can you play some George Brooks?
Or how 'bout a little Garth Jones?
Take me back to Tennessee,
won't you play one for me
Hey mister, play some Brooks and Jones

Well the singer raised the brim of his stetson
And he spoke in a kind forgiving tone
I don't mean no disrespect,
but I would suspect
You'd be thinkin' Garth Brooks and George Jones

So the drunk took a drink, and he stood up
And all the while, he leaned heavy on me
He was feelin' somewhat bolder,
with his hand on my shoulder
And I could tell, this was not gonna' be pretty

He said mister, you ain't no George Brooks
Well you may have the hat,
but you ain't got the looks
And since your voice don't go real low
Well mister, you ain't no Garth Jones

Well I guess that's the way it's always been
When you piss all your money away
If you live in a bar,
you ain't never goin' very far
And to the stars our apologies

Hey mister, can you play some George Brooks?
Or how 'bout a little Garth Jones?
Take me back to Tennessee,
won't you play one for me
Hey mister, play some Brooks and Jones ♪

Speech From The Throne

He climbs on board
The thunderbolt below
The chute rails rattle
And he'll soon yell "Go"

Hooves will explode
As the gate opens wide
He'll be betting his life
On an 8 second ride

He feels like a king
Like he's up on a throne
This venomous ton
Of muscle and bone

Adrenalin pumpin'
In the man and the beast
Twisting and turning
There'll be no retreat

It's a ton of bad temper
With trouble in mind
What hope for a cowboy
To win or survive ?

But to sit on the throne
Bareback or saddle
To face it alone
His monster he'll straddle

And how many horses live
Under this hood?
On wild horse or bull
It'll come to no good

Some say it's a death wish
That makes him want to try
Some say it's the glory
Or the adrenalin overdrive

But only those who dare
Can really know for sure
The supernatural feeling
That primeval surge

The way it must have felt
To chase buffalo herds
Over plains without fences
Or discouraging words

It's the way that you feel
When you look up so high
And read what the heavens say
In the sign language of sky

It's your life in an instant
Less than a moment in time
And you may relish the chance
Of a good day to die

So the cowboy climbed on
At the appointed hour
How audacious it seems
To have challenged such power

He rode well that day
Under the Mesquite sun
But in six seconds flat
He was bucked off and gone

In just six seconds flat
It was over and done
When Bodacious The King
Gave the speech from the throne

Tommy ♪

Tommy likes to play the spoons
every Saturday afternoon
Down where the locals gather
at the old Black Diamond Saloon
Now Tommy's lived around here
for just about 41 years
And he's seen a lot of things change
but he still likes the good ol' days

Tommy likes to have a smoke
and he'll join you for a glass of beer
He likes to tell the girls a joke
he likes to pull your other ear
Now he don't make excuses
he just lives the life he pleases
And I guess he's earned the right
after more than 70 years

But he remembers a time
back when he was in his prime
When he used to work the land
and he used to like to ride
Then the whole damn thing went wrong
and when the old farm house burned down
Well it was too late to start over
so he had to move to town

And Tommy likes to sing a tune
especially when you ask him to
He'll sing the old time standards
Bob Wills or Jimmy Rodgers
And Tommy doesn't want to go home
until the very end of the show
Ain't no better way to pass the time
makin' music with friends of mine

And Tommy's still a lady's man
he's loved her all his life
Never been a cheatin' heart
since he took her as his wife
And in the years that she's been gone
he remembers faded love
Tommy's still his lady's man
and she belongs to the stars above

Tommy likes to play the spoons
every Saturday afternoon
Down where the locals gather
at the old Black Diamond Saloon
And Tommy doesn't want to go home
until the very end of the show
Ain't no better way to pass the time
makin' music with friends of mine

Yes Tommy likes to play the spoons ♪

One Eagle's Feathers

One eagle's feathers
Sold somewhere today
Where did they come from
And whom will it pay?

And what kind of medicine
Will this money bring
If bad medicine was used
To steal them away?

The eagle teaches us
When she flies
To lift our vision
Up to the skies

In calm reflection
We may watch her glide
Our spirits may soar
When we see her fly

And what can be learned
From one eagle feather
And for one eagle's life
How would we treat one another?

For one eagle's feathers
And one person's heart
It is never too late
To make a new start

For one eagle's vision
May open our eyes
The eagle teaches us this
Everytime she flies

This Western Romance

"….Candles are bright
when they're burning
And so to a love do compare…"

Across The Mountains ♪

I guess I missed you this time
when I crossed over the mountains
You were on the road again
playin' with a country band
I was hoping that we'd find
a little time to spend together
And a little conversation
in the language of the heart

Like this song I am writing
when it all comes together
When the music feels just right
and the words begin to rhyme
Like a river finds its way
on down to the ocean
When two hearts first collide
and then melt in tenderness

Now winter is a-comin' on
I can see it in the sky
The trees are turning colour
and the summer birds have flown
And each time that I see you
you seem more beautiful to me
I'm afraid how much I want you
and how good this love can be

That's when love crosses over the mountains
and love sails over the sea
Deeper than the deepest ocean
that's how deep this love can be
To rise on the wings of eagles
up to the highest peak
That's where love can take us
darlin' if you'll love with me ♪

Brightest Star ♪

Mama always liked to tell the story
of how she came to meet the man she wed
The Second World War had barely ended
when the love of her life would begin

She grew up on the poor side of town
she always tried to hold her head up high
A singer and a dancer is what she dreamed to be
and she did what she could to survive

He grew up on the western plains
and he lived through them dirty dust bowl years
And he thought he'd try to find something better
than a harvest of them same old bitter tears

So he headed east at the end of the war
and he moved into that same old side of town
And he took a room in a house on the street
where the love of his life would be found

They didn't have a long time together
they were married short of twenty years
And when he died she had to start all over
and even though she cried some bitter tears

She sang oh how I love you
oh how I care
Of all the stars in heaven
yours will shine the brightest there

She's lyin' up there in a hospital bed
she's back on that same old side of town
And she seems at peace, and the good memories
they're the ones she likes to talk about

She said she'd like to go and see him again
and she told us of a dream she had last night
And in that dream, she sang these words for him
and I knew this was a song I had to write

She sang oh how I love you
oh how I care
Of all the stars in heaven
yours is still the brightest there ♪

Candles ♪

Candles are bright
when they're burning
And so to a love do compare
Love feels so right
to keep the flame alive
Like a candle you must handle with care

Love is a flower
gently blooming
Flowers need the sun and the rain
Love will shed tears
as it grows through the years
But with too many tears it may fade

Love can light your life
like a candle in the night
Love can bring you hope
and teach your heart to feel
And if you see the light
you will learn what's wrong from right
And you will understand
the way that true love feels

Candles are bright
when they're burning
And so to a love do compare
Love feels so right
to keep the flame alive
Like a candle you must handle with care ♪

Buffalo Gal Won'tcha ♪

Buffalo Gal won'tcha come home tonight
You've been gone so long
Buffalo Gal won'tcha come back home
Back where you belong

Buffalo Gal won'tcha come on home
You've been gone since June
Buffalo Gal won'tcha come back home
And dance me around the room

Now every day I hang around
And sing this sad ol' song
And every night I wonder gal
If you've been doin' me wrong

You said you'd go to Laramie
To buy some pretty lace
But Laramie's full 'o cowboys gal
Who'd love your pretty face

Buffalo Gal won'tcha come home soon
'Cuz I've been feelin' blue
And if you quit your runnin' gal
I swear I'll marry you

No one else can hold me close
Like you used to do
And no one could console me gal
If you said we're through

Now you're the only cowgirl
From here to Tennessee
Can rope 'n ride 'n shoot 'n drink
And love the likes of me

So Buffalo Gal won'tcha come back home
You've been gone since June
Buffalo Gal won'tcha come back home
And dance me around the room ♪

Cold Wind ♪

There's a cold wind blowin'
through this heart of mine
I feel a chill down deep in my bones
And there's a cold wind blowin'
through this house tonight
You left the door wide open
and you're gone gone gone

The roof will soon be leakin'
when the hard rain starts to fall
And the shutters will be shakin'
when them northers start to blow
How can I be forsaken
left to run this spread alone
Without your arms to hold me gal
this house is not a home

Your letter on the table
brought a tear drop to my eye
You said this farmin' and this ranchin'
just ain't your kind of life

We planted in the springtime
and I thought we had it all
But it's a bitter kind of harvest
when the tears begin to fall

You left me for the bright lights
of Memphis Tennessee
I hear you're playin' down in Nashville
and maybe New Orleans
Do you love that country music gal
more than you love me
I hope someday you see the light
and you'll come back to me

Why did you have to leave me
why did you have to go
Why did you have to leave me be
the last one to know
You left me for the bright lights
of Memphis Tennessee
That City of New Orleans
took you far away from me ♪

Goodnight Colorado ♪

Goodnight Colorado goodnight
I'll see you in my dreams…again
Oh the trail has been long
And the memory strong
Of the way that we loved back then

Goodnight Colorado goodnight
I'll hear you sing again tonight
Now my heartache is gone
But the memory lives on
Of the music we made back when

We sang so well together
I thought it would never end
But the cold wind out of the Rockies
Blew my heart away once again

You left me at last for another
I can't blame you for the ways of love
But you'll always be my Colorado
Though you're gone down to ol' Mexico

And sometimes when I'm listening
To the all night border radio
I still hear your voice a-callin' to me
Somewhere down in ol' Mexico

Goodnight Colorado goodnight
I'll hear you sing again... tonight
Oh the trail has been long
And the memory strong
Of the music we made back then

Goodnight Colorado goodnight
I'll see you in my dreams...again
Oh the heartache is gone
But my love still goes on
Goodnight Colorado goodnight ♪

Corazon de Chihuahua ♪

Corazon de chihuahua
corazon de mi amor
Her name is Sophia
it's her I adore
She waits by the window
for me to come home
And when I open the door
she'll bark and say
take me for a walk por favor

My pretty chihuahua
what more can I say
For you I grow fonder
with each passing day
My constant companion
forever I'll sing
Corazon de chihuahua
ay yi yi yi yi

When skies are all cloudy
she knows what to say
When I'm feeling blue
she knows what to do
She brings me the sunshine
in her own special way
She gives me her love
under heaven above
there's no other so true

Corazon de chihuahua
corazon de mi amor
Corazon de mi vida
it's you I adore

My faithful companion
forever I'll sing
Corazon de chihuahua
ay yi yi yi yi

Ay yi yi yi
Corazon de chihuahua
Ay yi yi yi
Corazon de mi amor

My pretty chihuahua
so happy and gay
Do you wait for your boyfriend
to come out and play
He'll soon cross the border
and after awhile
He'll run to your side
and together with pride
you'll howl at the moon

He lives north of the border
in the US of A
Where so many compadres
go to work every day
You met at the fairgrounds
it was love at first bite
On the old Rio Grande
in the sunset light
on a very special night

He's the dog of a rancher
and a ranchero's wife
He's a big border collie
on the Texican side

'Til the day that he met you
he was lonely inside
Now he waits for the night
when he runs to your side
in the Mexicana moon

My long haired chihuahua
what more can I do
I once had a sweetheart
who looked a lot like you
With big brown eyes
and a long shaggy mane
And when she drank much tequila
she'd bark and she'd sing

Ay yi yi yi
Corazon de chihuahua
Ay yi yi yi
Corazon de mi amor ♪

Love's Miracles, # 39

Love conquers all –
The skunk married the monkey
And their new born bundle of joy – a skunkey!

Seasick In The Saddle ♪

I'm seasick, in the saddle
and I'm thinkin' about the coast
Her love was like an ocean
and that's what I miss the most
But the memory of being lost at sea
is haunting me again
And I'm seasick in the saddle
thinkin' 'bout what might have been

We fell in love like lovers do
in the springtime of our lives
We laughed and played like dolphins
and we frolicked on the tide
'Til a sudden gale like a jealous whale
left our happy home capsized
Now I'm shipwrecked on the prairies
since she left me high and dry

I'm seasick, in the saddle
maybe lovesick I don't know
Or maybe I'm just homesick for my mama
back home in Ontario
Sometimes it seems that this ol' saddle
is such an empty place to be
And why I live this cowboy life
is still a mystery to me

I guess a sailor needs the ocean
like a cowboy needs the land
And a pirate guards his treasure
like a jealous married man
For there's different kinds of heartache
and different kinds of gold
And if laughter is good medicine
then love can feed the soul

Seasick in the saddle
such a crazy way to be
When there ain't a drop of water
as far as eyes can see
Still I wouldn't trade the life I live
for all those might have beens
I guess we live the life we've chosen
like a sailor sails the sea ♪

Take Care Of Her Heart ♪

When he walked into the tavern
I could tell right away
How the lines upon his face
told the wisdom of his age
And it wasn't very long
before we got to talkin'
And I found a change of heart
in a simple conversation

So I told him the story
of how we fell apart
How we never intended
to break each other's heart
And I could tell that he was listenin'
by the teardrop in his eye
And the words that he told me
somehow helped to change my mind

Take care of her heart
what else can you do
If it really was over
you'd find someone new
But you love her still
and you know that she loves you
So take care of her heart
and she'll take care of you

He said a heart needs attention
and a kind word everyday
Instead of findin' fault
instead of layin' blame
And love is like a garden
it will blossom over time
But if you take the rose for granted
it'll wither on the vine

As I drove back home alone that night
to the house we used to share
I just couldn't stand to think
that I wouldn't find you there
And the old man's words lingered
like a bell that rang so clear
So I stopped the car to call you
and tell you how I feel

Take care of your heart
what else can I do
If it really was over
I'd find someone new
But I love you still
and I know that you love me
So take care of my heart
and I'll take care of you

Take care of her heart
and she'll take care of you ♪

Like Diamonds And Pearls

Like diamonds and pearls
Suzanne
When I found you shining there
In those rough surroundings
Your talent, grace
And devotion apparent
To a thirsty soul like mine

For I have travelled many lands
Seen diamonds, pearls and shifting sands
And I myself must be by now
A stone less rough
My edges honed by the polisher's buff
As I've listened to voices, hearts and minds
In distant cultures so different than mine

I watch you tonight, like a diamond pearl
Playing pool in a honky tonk saloon
And somewhere past midnight
I bathe in this innocent desire
Your glow for me is like visual perfume
You do not need anyone to save you
From me, from life, your very own self

For you and I are like diamonds and pearls
Not dependent, but complementary
Our voices together make such music
Like birds of a feather, I am moved to ask
Where does such harmony belong
If not, like diamonds and pearls
In a treasure chest of song?

This Western Romance ♪

This western romance
Has nearly ended
Forget your tears, and the times we cried
A new day is dawning, and it's time to ride
'Cuz this western romance
Has all but died

Now you don't have to look so sad
We gave it all we had
We made mistakes I know
But it's time to let them go
And on the horizon, far as I can see
There'll be better times ahead for you and me

And when we started
Well I thought we'd make it
But when the fire got hotter
I knew I couldn't take it
Then the wind blew colder
And the flame burned lower
And I know that you and I
Aren't the kind who can fake it

Like a western movie, full of heroes
Who gamble on stakes so high
You know they're bound to lose it all
And in the final shoot-out
When the smoke had cleared
There was nothing left to lose
There was no doubt at all

This western romance
Has nearly ended
Forget your tears, and the times we cried
A new day is dawning, and it's time to ride
'Cuz this western romance
Has all but died

This western romance
Is pretty much fried ♪

New Mexico

Her velvet auburn hair
Is so rich and so deep
Like the color of your hills
And makes my eyes turn my head
That I may see once more and again
How beauty is revealed only to me

The colors that she wears
Are soft and strong
Like your desert gardens
Where I discover once more and again
How nature's bright blooms and pastels fade
In keeping with your seasons

Her eyes are like
The turquoise and teal
Of your winter sunset sky
And the bracelets and rings she wears
The silver strands that wind round and caress
The arms and hands I wish to hold

And I am like the ripened fruit
Which hangs from an ancient tree
Planted by Spaniards so long ago
In your almost unforgiving soil
An ageing seeker finding the poetry
Of your graceful mystic twilight

When The Chiles Come Back To Rellenos ♪

When the chiles come back to Rellenos
And the coyote howls at the moon
I will hold my chihuahua closer
And I will be thinking of you

When the chiles come back to Rellenos
My chihuahua will sing a new tune
When I hold you again my darling
By the light of the New Mexican moon

When the sun comes up in the morning
Over Sangre de Cristo again
And the desert lillies are blooming
All around old Santa Fe

I remember that night oh my darling
When we met at the Blue Corn Cafe
When you brought me a cold cervesa
And I watched how your dress did sway

My name is Rosa Maria you said
I'll be your waitress tonight
I recommend the chiles rellenos
For the chiles have just become ripe

And as I tasted the chile rellenos
I knew it was love at first bite
And when the sun came up the next morning
You said we are now man and wife

But I am an alien worker
And I follow the old Turquoise Trail
Keeping one step ahead of the border patrol
So that I may see you again

So remember me oh my darling
Remember me in your prayers
And please say for me a rosary
To keep me out of their jails

When the chiles come back to Rellenos
And the coyotes howl at the moon
I will hold you again my darling
By the light of the New Mexican moon

When the chiles come back to Rellenos
My chihuahua will sing a new tune
When I see you again my darling
By the light of the New Mexican moon ♪

Yellow Moon ♪

Yellow moon, yellow moon, so bright
it's good to see you tonight
Yellow moon, yellow moon, above
shine, for me and my love

You waltz across the sky so bright
it's no wonder that you smile
And the stars that sparkle by your side
are dancing in my eyes

Yellow moon, yellow moon, above
shine, for me and my love

I'll tell my love, just how I feel
and if I can count on you
For when you shine, my love will see
my pledge of love so true

Yellow moon, yellow moon, above
shine, for me and my love

I know this love was meant to be
and I've waited for so long
And in your light my love and I
will find where we belong

Yellow moon, yellow moon, so bright
it's good to see you tonight
Yellow moon, yellow moon, above
shine, for me and my love ♪

Summer Corn

The corn still feels warm, she says
From the heat of the summer's day
And we laugh at serendipity's alliteration
As she pulls the husks away

And as I lean way back
Into this old camp chair
I gaze into the sunset
And the colours in her hair

Tonight as we make camp
Beside this quiet little lake
We will roast the corn of summer
And love the night away

Thanks ♪

Thanks for the love,
under the moon and stars above
Oh how we've loved,
thanks for your love

Thanks for the kiss,
and moments just like this
And when we're apart,
it's you that I miss

Tears may fall and rain may fall
My whole world could turn to grey and blue
Moon will rise and sun will rise
And I'll still be dreaming of you

Thanks for the touch,
fits just like a glove
To know someone so well,
and love so much

Stars may fall and skies may fall
My whole world could turn to grey and blue
Moon will rise and sun will rise
And I'll still be dreaming of you

Memories and dreams,
starlight and moon beams
We're all made of this
Love is all there really is

Thanks for the love ♪

Places Of The Heart

"....Have you ever left your past behind
In search of open sky."

Alberta Blue ♪

Into the blue, Alberta Blue
I will follow you, Alberta Blue
Deep in the heart, wild and true
Into the blue, Alberta Blue

And when I have to go
somewhere down the road
And I'm carrying my shoulders
like some heavy load
I'll remember you, so wild and true
And the comfort of your love
is gonna' see me through

Into the blue, Alberta Blue
I've been missin' you, Alberta Blue

And when I'm on the road
and I'm someplace new
And I'm losin' my direction
and get to feelin' blue
I'll remember you, so wild and true
And the compass of your love
will bring me home to you

And if you ever go
somewhere down the road
And you're followin' that rainbow
to some pot of gold
When you think of me, and these wild blue eyes
And the comfort of my arms
and these endless skies

Into the blue, Alberta Blue
I will follow you, Alberta Blue
Deep in the heart, wild and true
Into the blue, Alberta Blue ♪

Montana ♪

I'm goin' back to old Montana
that's where I long to be
Montana Montana I've missed you
you've always been good to me
I'll make my home in old Montana
I guess it's my destiny
Montana Montana I love you Montana
you're the last great place to be free

From Dillon to Bighorn
from Billings to Great Falls
as far as eyes can see
Your mountains and rivers
your badlands and timbers,
stretch out eternally
Like many before me I came to explore
and find myself as a man
I wasn't the first and I won't be the last
to put my life and love in your hands

And some came to paint your western sky
some followed the buffalo
Some came seeking fortune
some came to save their souls

Some would call you paradise
some call you sacred ground
And somewhere above the Bighorns tonight
all souls are heaven bound

In a land where once the buffalo
roamed in herds untold
And the hunter became the hunted
in the bygone days of old
In the land of Gall and Crazy Horse
the Blackfoot, Sioux and Crow
Where the grizzly ruled his kingdom
in the land of the Yellowstone

I'd like to ride my pony once more
beneath your great big sky
From the prairies to the foothills
'til we reach the Great Divide
And when we cross the Shining Mountains
we'll be goin' to the sun
Like our fathers did before us
and our children still to come ♪

Chez LaVerne

Friday morning
Lazy late summer's breakfast
At LaVerne's Grill
Tucked away
In Garden Bay
Big City feels
So far from here

Nothing new
Under the sun
The four winds blow
And life goes on
In Pender Harbour
The tall trees dance
To the ocean's tune

Beautiful Country ♪

When I ride the Coquihalla
Up in the high country
The hills of the sagebrush and pine
Where the great Nicola Valley
Spreads out wide before me
And takes me back
To another state of mind

When the rangeland was wide open
And they used to drive the cattle
Up and down the trails
West of the Great Divide
This Land was made for cattle
And workin' in the saddle
Was a dream come true, this cowboy way of life

From the Thompson and Chilcotin
East to the Rocky Mountains
Down the Fraser Canyon
Out to the western sea
This land was opened up
By all kinds of people
People who just wanted to be free

And up in the high country
This beautiful country
Where the air is clean
And the view is always free
Where I became a cowboy
And if I had it my way
There ain't no other place I'd have to be

This land was made for horse and cattle
Long days and trails in the saddle
Round the campfire tonight
If the moon is shinin' bright
We're gonna' serve up every poem
And song we know
This cowboy life's the only way to go ♪

High Desert Moon

The moon will bloom in June
across the desert sky
The bloom of sage so fills the night
it's fragrance lifts the mind
To dream a dream of dreams again
of wild horse and rider
of cowboy love and lore
and days of the future
days gone forever
and days forevermore....
Across the high desert sky
in Oregon...
tonight

Calgary ♪

Calgary
Calgary
Your star is rising high and shines
for everyone to see
You've opened up the future
to opportunity
The jewel of the western sky
you've found your destiny

Calgary
Calgary
Born and bred in freedom
with a rugged history
You've opened up your doors
to welcome as a friend
Any woman, any man
with an honest hand to lend

Once you were a vision
of better things to come
The pioneers who founded you
had faith in what they'd done
Now you've seen a hundred years
you've finally hit your stride
Your silver towers touch the sky
and you wear success with pride

Nestled in the foothills
where the Bow river winds
Where the prairies kiss the Rockies
beneath the western sky
And though your people read the news
and maybe dress in city clothes
Beneath the finest three piece suit
still walks a western soul

Calgary
Calgary
Your star is rising high and shines
for everyone to see
You've opened up the future
to opportunity
The jewel of the western sky
you've found your destiny ♪

Let The Rockies Rock Me Tonight ♪

Snow started fallin'
late yesterday
Looks like a blizzard
I heard the weatherman say
Storm warnin's out
for at least another day
And here I am alone on this lonely highway
this lonely highway

Pulled out of Vancouver
late yesterday
Vancouver to Alberta
takes more than just a day

I've got to make a deadline and get to Calgary
it's more than just a job
There's a girl who waits there for me
I know she waits just for me

It's a long way from heaven
It's a longer way from home
High on this mountain
I've never felt more alone
But there's a peaceful kind of feelin'
falls with the fallin' snow
Here in this stillness
I will rest until I must go

But the snow's driftin' higher
and the drivin's gettin' harder
Guess I'll stop and wait
for the mornin' light
All alone in the Rockies
well it just don't seem right
To dream alone without you
let the Rockies rock me tonight
let the Rockies rock me tonight

Rock me tonight ♪

Fraser Valley ♪

I've travelled far and I've travelled wide
Seen the seven oceans,
I've crossed the great divide
I never expected to find myself here
Livin' in this valley, where the skies are so clear

Fraser Valley you look so good to me
Mountains surround you down to the sea
Room to be free and dance to a song
Fraser Valley you're the place, I belong

We all have our hard times along the way
But look how the sun, shines down on us today
I once was lost but now I'm free
And the sun shines bright enough,
for everyone to see

Fraser Valley you feel so good to me
Green pastures rolling down to the sea
Room to be free and dance to a song
Fraser Valley you're the place, I belong

I know I'd never find, if I looked everywhere
A place in the world that can compare
To the green of your fields,
and the blue of your sky
To the peaceful feeling,
in this good ol' heart of mine

Fraser Valley you've been so good to me
Room for my friends and family
Room to be free and dance to a song
Fraser Valley you're the place, I belong ♪

In Canada ♪

Oh the rain up here
Makes the trees grow tall
And the mountains high
Where the big snows fall
I asked my love
Come live with me
Out on the land
In Canada

Oh the rivers wind
And the salmon spawn
And a man depends
On a woman's love
Hand in hand we'll walk
Under stars above
In the land we love
In Canada

And the winds of change
Never changed our minds
Since we fell in love
On that starry night
And we walked among the pines
She and I
And I thank the Lord
For the stars above
And this life we live
That's been built on love
And our dreams that have come true
In Canada

Oh the rain up here
Makes the trees grow tall
And the mountains high
Where the big snows fall
I asked my love
Come live with me
Out on the land
In Canada

In the land we love – Canada ♪

On Ruby Lake

Looking west
On Ruby Lake
As sunset smiles
On all of us – people, turtles
Snakes, ducks and geese
All sunning ourselves
In mid-summer heat while
Violet-green and
Orange-breasted swallows
Weave and dance their
Airborne arias
To the strains of
Italian opera
As we dine like kings
And queens
In this open air
Wilderness
Trattoria

When enjoying
Fine dining
Such as this –
It is best to compose
Lightly

Mount Baker Serenade ♪

Well I'm goin' home today
I've worked so hard to make my way
And home in the valley, I know that I'll find
The peace that makes it all worthwhile

There's a family that waits just to greet me
And friends that are always nearby
There's a feeling of freedom, here in the valley
To the hills that reach up to the sky

Mount Baker watches over, like a solitary soldier
Protecting the dreams of the free
And I know that the future,
depends on the children
And they're depending on you and me

Well a man has to find his future
No matter where he's come from
And with the comfort of love,
he can rise above
The failure that once stood in his way

Yes a man has to find his heaven
No matter what hell he's been through
And a man needs a woman,
to help him believe in
The life he's been given to lead

So together let's build our future
As we follow the river of life
'And we'll learn how to live,
how to share and to give
And nothing can take that away

171

Mount Baker watches over, like a solitary soldier
Protecting the dreams of the free
And I know that the future,
depends on the children
And they're depending on you and me –

For a lullaby, at the close of their day ♪

San Diego ♪

I'm goin' home, to San Diego
Where the sun is warm and fine
And my family will greet me, tenderly
And the palm trees soothe my worried mind

Yes it's hard to leave this valley
And to leave my friends behind
But the ocean breeze is callin', to me
Whispering, now's the time

Oh my thoughts drift back to that cantina
Senorita, I had to leave behind
And the mariachi band that played there
South of the borderline

Although there's a border between us
We're only a moment apart
Someday we'll sail that sea together, you and I
In each ending there's always a new start

And you will always be here in my heart ♪

Open Sky ♪

I said goodbye to my closest friends
and to my next of kin
I had to leave a lot behind
to let this dream begin
Sold it all and I drove out west
just following the sun
Back to the land where I feel my best
out where the west was won

I said goodbye to yesterday
and set out on my way
I just don't think I'll ever take
that same old road again
I've got a mind to find myself
out on the western plains
Between the eagle and the dove
where the deer and coyote play

Have you ever seen Montana
or watched an eagle fly
Ever crossed Wyoming
underneath the pale moonlight
Have you ever loved Alberta
how she changes with the wind
Have you ever left the past behind
in search of open sky?

I left her standing at the door
she turned her head away
To hide the tears that we both felt
and nothing more to say
Maybe she'll join me when I figure it out
what it is I'm looking for
If she'll forgive this restless soul
and we can find a dream once more

But she's never seen Montana
or watched an eagle fly
Never crossed Wyoming
underneath the pale moonlight
But she reminds me of Alberta
how she changes like the wind
And someday we'll leave the past behind
in search of open sky

Have you ever left your past behind
in search of open sky? ♪

Red River Plains ♪

I heard my first country song
on the Red River plains
West of the Mississippi
a sky full of rain
Heard the steel guitars ring
and I listened to the fiddle bow
How I loved the sound that I found
on a one channel radio

I remember Eddy Arnold
and his lonesome cattle call
And when Frankie Lane sung that ol' mule train
I figured I'd heard it all
I remember times up among the pines
when I heard that coyote call
Take me back in time down the line
where the Red River flows

And when the snow started melting
there was water all around
In the spring of '97
no refuge could be found
From Texas to Manitoba
they're gonna' have to start again
They're the farmers and the ranchers on
the Red River plains

I've seen a lot of empty faces
on the streets of this old town
Sad and lonely traces
of a dream broken down
I need them wide open spaces
where a man can see for miles
Like my father walked before me
under the Red River skies

White lightenin' strikes above me
shootin' stars start to fall
When the northern lights come dancin'
and the Red River flows
Every now and then I remember when
I heard that ol' train whistle blow
Take me back in time until I find
where the Red River flows ♪

Royal Canadian Sunset

The Rockies are mostly blue and gray
On this late day in May
And against the early evening sky
They still wear their snowy caps
All dressed in white and tails
They stand in line at sunset
In honour they parade
Awaiting Her Royal Majesty
Their mountain queen
The queen of their every night

Alberta Serenade ♪

You know I think about you when I'm gone
Even though it didn't work out like we planned
This work that I've taken on the coast
Only lets me come to see you
Now and then, now and then

You know I'd like to live out on your land
Maybe when my ship comes in someday
It's those long lonely winters I can't stand
But we could spend them down near Phoenix
Now and then, now and then

I'd like to settle down with you someday
We could do all those things just like we planned
If these songs that I write will ever pay
And if they don't I'm still the lucky man,
you understand

Alberta please
I've loved you for so long
Underneath your sunny skies
I'm back where I belong
Alberta please
Hold me closer in your arms
And underneath the stars above
I'll fall in love with you again ♪

Rocky Mountain Time ♪

I've been out on the east coast
to see the Maritimes
I took a ride on a fishin' boat
and I travelled down the line
I've seen a lot of highway
Nova Scotia to Ontario
But tonight I'd like to take this flight
to my Rocky Mountain home

I've been out on the west coast
up to the timberline
I took a ride on a sailin' boat
and I travelled down the line
I've seen a lot of highway
Alaska down to Mexico
But tonight I'd like to take this flight
to my Rocky Mountain home

Well it's hard to paint a picture
when your pallet has run dry
And it's hard to tell a story
if you've never wondered why
And it's hard to write a song
if you've never felt the need to roam
It's hard to keep on goin'
when the spirit doesn't want to go

I've seen this land from coast to coast
and so I've come to know
You take the worst and you take the best
and reap what you have sewn
Sometimes it's hard to know just what you've lost
until you've let it go
Like a ship without an anchor
and a man without a home

I'm gonna' set my watch on
Rocky Mountain time
Let this big bird
take me home
across the great divide
And when I touch the ground
I'll be on Rocky Mountain Time ♪

Saskatchewan ♪

Grandaddy settled down
About a hundred years ago
In a land that was called Saskatchewan
Grass was high and the sky was blue
He said there ain't much here
But we'll make it do
I think I've found a home
Saskatchewan

England seemed so long ago
When he rode that west bound train
And them rules and regulations
Of Britannia slipped away

179

And to look out across the plain
Makes a man feel big inside
Underneath the western sky
Saskatchewan

It's never been an easy life
For a woman and a man
To make a living on the land
In Saskatchewan
But to see those northern lights
And the wild bird take to flight
In the magic of the land
Saskatchewan

Cross the border and I wonder why
I ever felt the need to roam
Now at last I'm comin' home
Saskatchewan
It might be hard to explain
How the wisdom of the plains
Pass from the fathers to the sons
In Saskatchewan

The mighty herd of the buffalo
So few of them remain
And like the old ways of the plains
Barely hangin' on
But the legends live forever
And the people carry on
And winter's come and gone
In Saskatchewan

And a new day has begun
In Saskatchewan ♪

Yellowhead Highway ♪

I'm drivin' the Yellowhead Highway
I'll take her as far as she goes
Out west to the mighty Pacific
Back home to the wild prairie rose

Some say the road goes on forever
Some say the party never ends
But darlin' you and I we both know better
And I can't wait to see you again

I've seen the sunrise on the mountains
I've seen the sunset on the sea
From Saskatoon to old Prince Rupert
Your voice is callin' to me

I've seen my picture in the mirror
The lines mark the changes and the miles
But the one thing that always keeps me goin'
Is the fountain of youth in your smile

Some days I don't know where I'm goin'
Some days I don't know what to do
Somehow we keep the fire burnin'
And this Yellowhead's gonna' bring me home to you

I'm drivin' the Yellowhead Highway
I'll take her as far as she goes
Out west from the mighty Pacific
Back home to the wild prairie rose ♪

Somewhere In The Rockies ♪

Somewhere in the Rockies
is where I want to be
Way up high where the eagles fly
and the air is clean and free
Now some might call me crazy
but I'd just call it destiny
Livin' up here on the top of the world
is just about right for me

From Santa Fe to Denver
Missoula to Cheyenne
From Calgary down to Laramie
the mighty Rockies stand
And you can drive highway 25
up to 90 and 93
Just takin' a ride on the Great Divide
can set your spirit free

I don't care how long it takes
I'm goin' back some day
And I won't need to count the cost
there is no price I wouldn't pay
The best of plans may fall apart
and lead you far astray
But when you listen to your heart
you'll surely find a way

The Rocky Mountains roll along
in all their majesty
Down south by old El Paso
To the Northern Mystery
Up where the wide Missouri
and the mighty Rio Grande
Start their journeys to the sea
from Nature's high command

Somewhere in the Rockies
is where I'll always be
Even in my dreams at night
the spirit's callin' me
To the land of the Shining Mountains
until my race is run
Somewhere in the Rockies
goin' to the sun ♪

Now And Zen In The West

"….Haiku noon
The old west meets the old east –
Guess who become one?"

Awestruck

Summer thunderstorm
Lightening strikes
Me – awestruck as usual

Conversation With An Owl

Hello…I write haiku
And what do you do? –
Whooo!

Old Santa Fe

The naked winter trees
Cannot hide the magic of moonlight
In old Santa Fe – tonight

Effortless Contemplation

I step out for a walk
One early spring afternoon
The sun is bright
And scattered clouds
Suspend above
I hear the cry
Of an eagle –
One
Then two or more
I look up and find
Three, four and more in flight
They circle above
They seem to glide
Effortlessly
In contemplation
Of their field of vision

I maintain my gaze
Upward…above
This verdant coast where
They fulfill their life command
As I do mine
And I am reminded
Of the field of vision
Which opens to
Effortless contemplation –
And all the while I watched them
Before they disappeared
From my sight
I did not once see
Any one of them
Flap their wings
Or do anything… but soar

Full Moon Now

Full moon shines
Into my open tent window
3:05 am
With six banded beams
Of translucent light
Broadcasting silently from Moon Central
In hexagonal directions
Like an ancient insignia
Of Nature itself
Before religion took hold
It is just as it is
And we dream our dreams

Full moon stands alone
Above the low bank
Of ethereal cloudy mist
Holding silently over
The shrouded lake below
Awakened – I see
How fortunate I am
Alive and aware
Of Nature itself
Before and after religion
It is just as it is
Full moon – now

Haiku Noon

The ego loves to die
When pierced –
By the bullet of it's own truth

        Showdown at haiku noon –
          The old west guns down
            The inventors of gunpowder

At haiku noon –
  The old martial artist
    Dances round the old marshal

        At haiku noon
        The old west meets the old east –
        Guess who become one?

Manna

One man's manna –
another man's manure

One woman's compost –
another woman's cure

One woman's garbage –
another man's grace

One man's fantasy –
another woman's fate

One woman's junk –
another woman's joy

One man's crucifix –
another man's toy

Do we often fill up
perfect emptiness
with garbage?

Nightmare

Look at the moon, honey!
That's not the moon, dear –
It's the new walmart sign
In Madeira Park

One Cow's Haiku

The brahma bull
Waiting patiently –
To have its toenails clipped

On The Origin Of Cow Haiku

I hear tell we've got
Japanese rodeo riders
Now
So it figures –
We will soon see
The cross-breeding
Of Rodeo
With Zen
And a new poetry genre
Which might be named –
Shall we say –
Cow Haiku?

Oops –
Looks like
We're already here
And – now!

Open Range – Open Mind

When you look out across the plains
As far as the eyes can wander
It becomes possible to imagine
The way it must have been
On a range wide open
In a land without borders

But if your heart is defended
By barbed wire fences
If your soul has been branded
By yesterday's losses
And your mind is so closed
Like it's gone out of business

You'll just drive right through here
On the high road to nowhere
On a highway to hades
Stuck in the past
Or afraid of the future
Without a care for what is always right here

We are Westerners
We ain't stuck livin' in the past
We just happen to prefer living
Where the wind sends waves
Through an ocean
Of tall prairie grasses

We are Westerners
We are drawn to these places
Where minds may dream
And hearts may know
The magic of skies
And wide open spaces

For the open range is a state of mind
The way it's always been
You become what you believe
And you may live in regret
Or learn to ride with the changes
Where the wide open mind
finds those wide open ranges

Summer Haiku

Death Of The Dragon

And who catches the dragonfly?
The same one with wings –
Who sings so sweetly at sunset

Summer Camp

Summer camp –
Happily surrounded – I surrender
To berries, jays and blue sky

Floating

Under blue summer sky
Over still waters –
My floating raft and I

Jay's Blues

Such a beautiful blue coat
Such a scolding tone of voice
The jay bird sings the blues

Outstanding Insights

Outstanding insights may come to you
If you have been so long
Outstanding in your field
That you find yourself wondering
About the following kinds of questions –

What is an open range?
What if an open range is a state of mind?
What if an open range is an open mind?
What if an open mind leads to an open range?
And what the hell is an open mind?

What if the universe is an open range?
What if an open range is a quiet mind?
What if open range is awareness of all?
What if open mind is pure awareness?
What if the universe is an open mind?

And why are cows outstanding in their field?
And what if cows have quiet minds?
And why are cows so patient?
And what if cows started writing poems?
What would such poems be called?

Is life an endless multiple-choice test?
And are there any answers, wrong or right?
Is there a time for every porpoise, under heaven?
Well, maybe cows have some insight
into such questions
They've been outstanding in your field, after all

Three Cow Haikus

A cow poem
is naturally –
a moozing to us

And if a moo is how
a cow makes haiku –
can we not make haiku too ?

By this kind of logic –
can we not all be
amoozingly bovine haiku poets?

seagull

I watch the seagull as she flies
Where'er she goes there so do I

I watch the clouds passing by
I see them change and so do I

I feel the wind caress my skin
It comes and goes and so do I

I find the sun and moon and stars
Where'er they roam there so do I

I know all creatures great and small
Here they belong and so do I

I watch the seagull cross the sky
She knows I'm with her, as she flies

May all beings live their own heart's song
We all belong – for we are one

The Cowboy Met The Buddha

The cowboy met the buddha
Somewhere west of east
Somewhere way out on the trail
In search of some kind of peace

It was once upon a time
While ridin' that endless fence line
Where the mind begins to wander
'Til there's no such thing as time

It was once upon such a day
In dreams of open range
He came upon a lone stray
Or so it seemed at first anyway

There under a cottonwood tree
A burst of unusual color
Orange as an autumn day
This one late day in spring

Orange was the color
Of the robe the stranger wore
Sittin' under that cottonwood
The cowboy could not ignore

Hey Mister…you over there
You sittin' under that tree
What are you a-doin'
On this here private property?

The man didn't answer in words
Or turn his head around
He simply plucked a single dandelion
And twirled it gently 'round

Now the cowboy was curious
For as he could plainly see
This weren't no Smith & Wesson
Nor other firearm piece

It was a single barrelled flower
Held out like a palm leaf
Gentle as a fawn it spoke
Of innocence and peace

So how'd you get out here?
The cowboy thought to ask
And where are you a-goin'
In this land so west of east?

The stranger seemed to speak
Although it could have been the wind
The clouds above began to sing
The music of a hymn

And the leaves of the cottonwoods
Began to rustle in the wind
Like echoes of his childhood
Which came right back to him

So the cowboy spread his bedroll
Under that cottonwood tree
He stoked an evening fire
And he cooked a meal of beans

For the evening sky spoke of peace
At the end of another day
The sun was slowly sinkin' low
And the wheel would turn again

He used to think in two dimensions
Like there's only black or white
And he had done a lot of wrong
In try'n to prove that he was always right

He let go of a load that night
He just stopped worryin'
He saw that when he holds on too tight
He just adds to the suffering

The seasons change and life goes on
So why not let it be
It's just mother nature doin' her thing
So what is there to fear

Yes the cowboy met the buddha
Somewhere west of east
And he let go of an ego load
On the road to inner peace

On A Good Day

It is a good day to die
and a good day to live
and the enlightened one
knows
the difference
is nil
where –
it's all good –
beyond
the
one
mind
divided

The Enduring West

"….Don't you ever fear
We will still be here
No matter how things change
We remain the same
We are the Cypress Hills."

Centennial Wind

The wind's been blowing across this land
and ever since time began
It's carried away most everything
that could not learn to bend
While those with wings can fly away
'til spring returns again
It's those who stay to plant the seed
and those who've seen a hundred years
Who know the full measure of joy and pain
and reasons why we celebrate
this first Centennial

More than a hundred summers ago
my great grandfather's solitary plough
first broke the earth of these northern plains
With Sitting Bull and Riel just barely gone and
Big Bear, Poundmaker and Piapot grown old,
and silently
the buffalo all but vanquished
like summer wheat to the sudden cold
The time for each of us to harvest is short
and live life to the full
For the winds of fate may blow away
anything we try too hard to hold

And who will hear the wind blow
a hundred years from now
And whom of us will live to see
a hundred summer suns
And who will tell the stories
of how it all began

And how will wisdom so hard won
reflect in works which we have done
And who will know and understand
how far we've really come
when the next Centennial comes around

Then shall we not leave something wild and free
the way it was when first seen
by our great grandfathers and mothers
and our First Nations sisters and brothers
Even here within this city's heart
let us leave something natural, clean and clear
For the earth is ours not to own
but to honour and bestow
And for our children and great grandchildren
when future generations behold
the coming again of the Centennial Wind

And the wind brings the time
of the harvest
And the wind brings
the long winter cold
And the spring comes in
like a welcome old friend
And the warm winds of summer
make me smile
And our stories are told by and by
like a thread into the new millennium
as we celebrate our first Centennial

Timepiece

Time passes when you're busy
and whether you're not
Time may not help you remember
the things you forgot
Time marches on
and may leave you behind
But if you're a lucky one
time may seem kind

Time passes quickly
for those who are busy
And doesn't much matter
to those who are lazy
Time follows the beat
of nobody's drum
Whether you're old
or whether you're young

Your name might be Caesar
Napoleon or Gall
Marilyn Munroe or Kennedy
it doesn't really matter at all
For time will outlive you
and time doesn't rust
See the works of Ozymandias
it has withered into dust

But time is an old friend
to a cowboy on the range
And anyone who knows
there's nothing to blame
When you follow your calling
Or you live on the land
So close to the earth
well ain't it just grand!

October Again ♪

Moon on the rise in the eastern sky
Sun goin' down in the west
Sunset on the Rockies
Is the time I love the best

Some of these hills are a golden brown
Some of them trees are bare
Patches of green still can be seen
Traces of snow here and there

Now it's work all day in a field of hay
'Til harvest is pretty much done
Tomorrow we'll go and find them strays
Round-up's just begun

Two weeks ago we had our first snow
And the mercury fell to the floor
Now it's back again and the big chinook
Keeps winter from our door

I like to ride up in the hills
And look out across the plains
I feel a sense of wonder for
My home out on the range

It's October again
In the foothills
It's a time of change
Everywhere
Well the leaves will fall
And the wind will howl
And the coyote sings on the range
It's October in the foothills once again ♪

210

Beneath The Arch

The sun descends
Beneath the arch
On a mid-October's day
And all the world is set aglow
Before the evening shade
As autumn grasses glisten
Like golden tears before the rain
While leaves of burning orange
And distant mountains loom
Like foreshadows of a coming cold

The moon rises among
Silent thinning clouds
In a docile eastern sky
The silhouettes of summer
Like whisps of vapour disappearing
And as I stand and watch
The passing of a day
Beneath the arch I fall
In love and rise again
Like every passing heartbeat

Culture On The Range

What is cowboy culture, I heard him ask
and how did it begin and where
And how far would you have to travel
to find any of it way the hell out here?

Well wait a minute, says I –
after all doesn't it kind of depend
On how you might define the word
and whether friend or foe

Out here on the western range
it's really no mystery to see
How culture comes down through the ages
of our western history

For culture is what we do
when we're sittin' around the fire
It's the stories told by flames of gold
that keep the West alive

Culture is also what we do
when we drive five hundred miles
To bring a herd to market, or come to a gatherin'
To read a poem or sing a song or two

And it's stayin' up half the night and more
with a guitar in one hand
And another cold beer or three
Or waitin' for a brand new calf, to be born free

And if there's still another log for the fire
so more stories can be told
And the circle of life in all it's grace
can naturally unfold

So the young 'uns can find their feet
and learn to stand up on their own
That's when you know there's culture
and another job well done

So if you've come to paint
this fabled western sky
Or just to live out on the prairies
and along the Great Divide

Culture is everything we do
that brought us here and keeps us here
It's what we do and pass along
it's a living legacy

Culture is life lived in recognition
of life's great mystery
No matter where you happen to be
but 'specially when you know you're free

And you'll pick a song or read a poem
without askin' for a great big fee

56 Summers

On this last day of august
The waning summer sun
Still warms an ageing soul
In this my summer of 56
My 56th year
For 56 summer suns have I seen –
More than Mozart
Alexander The Great
Custer
Keats
Terry Fox
Martin Luther King
More than Sitting Bull
My own father
The Children of Africa
And so many more –
We all may die
But how many of us
With some awareness
Or the chance to tell
Someone something
Of how we have truly lived?

Grant MacEwan's Cabin

We spent an afternoon
at Grant MacEwan's cabin
Up in the bush past Sundre
on a sunday late in august, 2004

We gathered at Grant's old cabin
family, friends and rounders like me
A celebration, reunion, an inclusion –
all welcome home, in peace

We hung out on the sundeck
facing west in the afternoon sun
Overlooking a quiet river valley
as Grant had planned so well

And when storm clouds gathered quickly
and brought the rain and a chill
We retreated into the cabin
and shared our songs and warm smiles

Grant had built this cabin I am told
alone, without even hammer and nails
I cannot imagine what it took –
I just relaxed into the peace I felt

Perhaps Grant was one of those –
larger than life, of whom tales are told
But I am richer for the quiet space he built
and that's just the way Grant would have wanted it

Oh Ye Beautiful Stars

Oh ye beautiful stars
I wonder
Will ye seem so far away
When I am gone from here
And if I join you up there
In the heavens where
We may roam around – together

Tonight as I watch
Ye seem so far away
And tomorrow
Who knows –
Shall I be
A closer neighbour to thee
In galaxies of heavenly being

Oh ye beautiful stars
Shining up above
It naturally makes us wonder
Who we really are –
As we look into your patterns
And find our imagined worlds
And dreams of heaven pure

Simply seeing you
Seeming so far away
Conveys to us
A vastness
That we must be
Intrinsically part of –
So much greater than,
little concepts of ourselves

Great Plains Of Heaven ♪

Every time I cross the plains
rolling hills of green and grain
I think about days gone by
and the ones who came before me
Back in 1885
my grandaddy and kin arrived
They settled on the sacred ground
the great northern prairie

The lost herd of the buffalo
the people of the horse and bow
The ranchers and the farmers
and the redcoats not forgotten
Somewhere east of the Cypress Hills
Major Walsh and Sitting Bull
Gallantly they tried to build
a bridge of understanding

And high above the clouds below
it never rains and it never snows
And the sun shines all the time
in a clear blue sky
And I wonder if anybody knows
where it is that we all go
When we finally cross the last medicine line,
medicine line

The dance hall looks full tonight
the evening stars are shining bright
People come from miles around
to hear the country music
I step outside and I look around
my thoughts are heaven bound
I wonder if they hear a sound
I wonder if they're listening

And I wonder if
there's a prairie up in heaven
High above the clouds
where the sun shines all the time
And I wonder if
they're all up there listening
Somewhere
on the great plains of heaven

Tonight
on the great plains of heaven ♪

Planting Of The Seed

The farmer clears the land
Of rock and stump and weed
In solemn preparation for
The planting of the seed

The farmer plants his seed
Of various kith and kind
In hopeful anticipation of
A harvest for his needs

The farmer teaches the son
To continue in these ways
And so tradition becomes the harvest
When the seedling plants the seed

As a teacher may plant the seed
In a young child's mind
Good planting may allow
The harvest to be kind

But how to plant and what
Are the questions which employ us
To avoid the bitter fruit
Of a careless heart's harvest

As in the ways of nature
And in the works of woman and man
Life unfolds in every deed
And every tiny planted seed

Ode To The Wild Turkey

In ancient old Turkey
the peacock ran asunder
when Alexander the Great
first went over there to plunder

And though the indigenous turkey
might surely have preferred
to hear of early CIA plans
to carve up the dear old bird

There arose a feathered firmament in the land
when on local radio a catchy song was heard
as Sam the Sham and the Pharaohs first
the great secret revealed,
good tidings to all, for the bird is the word

Like all of us in recent times for sure
who might have slept a whole lot more sound
if Barbara Bush had only preferred
to always sleep alone, with a Colt 45 in hand

Hunted from Maine to old Singapore
the Hindu Kush mountains, to the Oregon shores
the indomitable bird has such a will to survive
and it's only complaint is that it cannot really fly

The wild turkey is indeed a good and noble bird
and from ancient times and on, it's destiny assured
from the Bosporus Straits to old Plymouth Rock
with cranberry and gravy, is it annually served

Good Works Of The Lord ♪

Drivin' down this highway
westbound from Calgary
Skies are blue above me
and fields are turnin' green
The Rockies rise before my eyes
like the steeples of a church
And I feel like I'm a-watchin'
The Good Works of The Lord

And why did Charlie Russell
come to paint the western sky?
And why did Wild Bill Cody build
a home on the Yellowstone?
And why did Crazy Horse and Gall
fight for all that it was worth?
It must have been their visions of
The Good Works of The Lord

I've seen the Shining Mountains
I've crossed the desert sands
The bottomlands of Nevada
And the mighty Rio Grande
From the blue grass of Kentucky
to the Gulf of Mexico
I just never tire of witnessin'
The Good Works of The Lord

For to help a young one find her way
along this rocky road
And to help a stranger like a friend
with his wearisome heavy load

From the coast of Nova Scotia
to the shores of Oregon
May we plant the seeds of kindness
The Good Works of the Lord

For there ain't no walls near as high
beneath the western sky
Like the Rock of Ages standing tall
along the Great Divide
And the evening stars which shine above
light up the Church tonight
Out here in the great wide open –
The Good Works of The Lord ♪

Return Of A Westerner

He was born with one short leg
and one weak arm
About as bad as it can get in 1915 Saskatchewan
And because he couldn't ride nor rope so well
The sense of failure began to hurt like hell
And though he didn't want to let the family down
He knew he'd never make it out there,
on that family farm

He had to find some other way
to make his mark and earn his pay
He was quick and smart
and he could write and read
And in that county
there was still a cryin' need

For a teacher of all the twelve school grades
And so in a one room schoolhouse
he soon became
The local teacher of 'em all,
at just seventeen years of age

Well the pay was short and the days were long
And since his imagination couldn't help
but carry on
He soon set his mind on a medical education
But as times were tough
in the great depression
And there wasn't any money
where he came from
He knew he'd never make it through
that Winnipeg medical school

Then the war came along
and turned his attention
And to serve his country became
his prime motivation
But due to the aforesaid physical limitations
He couldn't live up to the military obligations
Where with one short leg and one weak arm
The cards were stacked too high against him

So he moved to the big city
and he worked in office towers
Though after work he always went
to just tendin' flowers
'Til the big war ended,
and he thought he'd settle down

Caught by circumstance in a big eastern town
And there didn't seem much sense
in just movin' down the line
As jobs were few and food was scarce
in the temper of those times

But in that short life he soon found the gold
The music of life in a young woman's voice
They married and struggled,
'til his death did them part
And because of their love, as short as it was,
Two fine young'uns were born and raised,
And both went west for good
when they became of age

He had tried to move us back west
in the early fifties
And as we visited the family farms
south of Yorkton
That's when I first laid eyes
on my western heritage
Rode a big white horse
and my uncle's John Deere
Right there I could have died and gone to heaven,
for sure
But somehow I knew that I was already there

But heaven didn't wait,
'cause the government called him back
Back to the big city,
and the guaranteed pay check
Where he knew he could keep the family fed
And with one short leg and one weak arm,
who could lay blame
For life had dealt him a short hand,
and in that big eastern city
He gave it all he had 'til the mid-sixties,
when he died there at the age of fifty

I imagine he'd have been happier
to never leave the land
Keepin' bees and teachin' young 'uns out there
in Saskatchewan
Perhaps that's why I'm drawn back to this place
Backtrackin' in his footsteps,
to where it all began
Back on the Great Plains,
where the circle finds completion
He's finally made it home through his kids,
because of everything he's given

Where Do We Go From Here ?

Where do we go from here, my friend
Oh where do we go from here?
When the family farm is so hard pressed
And two incomes aren't always nearly enough
Oh where do we go from here?

There seems enough oil in the ground, they say
And there seems enough blue in the sky
But where do we go you and I my friend
To follow our very own dreams
Oh where do we go from here?

Like those young prairie gals Joni and KD
With windblown hearts and restless minds
Where there was a song they soon found a way
And when they sang Help Me and Craving
Turned troubles into mere bus stops
along life's highway

So where do we go from here, my friend
And what do we do with our 'one precious life'
How far do we follow our very own dreams
And at what bus stop do we leave
our troubles and fears behind
And where do we go from here?

Under These Same Stars

Tonight – one last time
Camping under these stars
In late August I reflect –
I've had a wonderful life

Under these same stars
As a child I've made camp
Like one of the Group of Seven
on the Laurentian Shield
Entranced and humbled by all we beheld

Under these same stars
Barely into my twenties
Camping on Pacific beaches
The wisdom of Oriental Masters
on the tip of my eager tongue

Under these same stars
Have I camped on the Great Plains
Those entralling nights spent
Listening to coyote choirs in the Cypress Hills

Under these same stars
Have I grown from a boy to a man
And yet somehow, I reflect –
What more do I know,
than when my worldly life began?

For under these same stars
I am still the child enthralled –
And in these moments in the universe tonight
It seems forever, a wonder-full life

River ♪

Running deep to a distant shore
Following some high command
Carrying your share and more
Ancient arm of the hinterland

Winding with the march of time
Carving out a destiny
In your wandering you will find
What you're searching for

Oh river of my mind
Understand these troubled times, we live in
Oh river of my life
Take this soul, into the light

Like this river I need to be
Free to move until I see
Ocean sky and shining sand
The inner gift of a guiding hand

And there's a river inside of me
Carving out my destiny
Take this muddy water to the sea
And leave me, in harmony

Oh river of my mind
Understand these troubled times, we live in
Oh river of my life
Take this soul, into the light

Oh river of my mind
Understand my life's design
Oh river of my life
Take this soul, into the light ♪

Winter Turns To Spring ♪

Time, has a way of movin' on
You turn around one day and wonder,
where it's gone
And love, has a way of sometimes goin' wrong
If you take a love for granted, she'll be gone

And life, has a way of movin' on
But winter has a way of hangin' on,
much too long
'Til the cares of yesterday will melt away
In the warm spring rain, and the summer sun

And I've been away from you so long
But love has a way of hangin' on,
growin' stronger
And the day when I can hold you once again
Will be the day, when my winter turns to spring

When this winter turns to spring
gonna' see what time brings
When April turns to May
and these clouds roll away
When these fields turn to green
and I see you again
Then love will bloom again
when my winter turns to spring ♪

229

Coast Song

This is my coast song
And actually
It is as much a poem –
For these words appear
As if from nowhere
Like islands in the mist
And as I feel my way
My heart sings
In an ocean of music
On a sea of waves
In a sky moving
Each cloud
Reflecting a moment
Of life – passing by

Words first appear
Like phantoms
From distant islands
In the mind
They emerge and loom
Before me until
They seem to stand
Like rock and earth
In an ocean of music
In a sea of tides
Like thoughts
And emotions
They form and then
Are sometimes washed away

A poem is like land
An island in the sea
The music of the ocean
Flows round and surrounds
Embracing words
Erasing
Dissolving
Swirling
Embedding
Until a poem
Comes to rest
Like treasure
In the depths
Of my seeing

The Rustling

I hear the wind as it blows
across the Cypress Hills
The maple birch and elm
the rustling of the leaves

I wonder where it travels
this vagabond western wind
To whom does it beckon
what tidings will it bring

I lay awake all night long
beneath the western stars
I listened to the sounds
of prairie near and far

A coyote sang on distant hill
and cattle bawled nearby
Like crystal voices in the night
they pierced the silent sky

And long before the winter cold
conquers all the plains
And long before the blood runs cold
on a prairie winter's day

A summer wind still warms the land
on this september morn
The leaves of autumn turning gold
across Saskatchewan

The birds still sing their summer song
this Indian Summer's day
I found three red wing feathers
laid down beside my bed

The winds of autumn soon will blow
and clouds will gather nigh
Harvest time will come and go
and cowboy round-up time

I may never know exactly why
or if it all makes perfect sense
I just love it out on this prairie
where the magic never ends

I hear the wind as it blows
across the Cypress Hills
The maple birch and elm
the rustling of the leaves

In The Dreaming West

From February through April, 2005
The world stopped – in alarm
50 or more bald eagles found
Dead – decapitated, de-taloned
Near the Cates Park nesting ground
In North Vancouver, B.C. –
Hunted illegally for the dollars they bring
What kind of medicine is born of such sin?
And when any of us have lost our way
Would we do such things –
In desperation, revenge, in greed
Would we make such war, instead of peace?

Friday, December 12, 2003
The world stopped – in joy
50 Plains Bison set free again
On the Old Man On His Back
Prairie and Conservation Area
In southwest Saskatchewan –
Genetically pure
Descendants of the great herds
And it just feels good to see them run free
It's what we want to be part of –
It is life nurturing, fulfilling
It is our vision – dream, coming true

The Cypress Hills ♪

The moon is full on this september night
In the Cypress Hills
The stars are bright in the prairie sky
Above the Cypress Hills

Summer's come and gone
And so are you my love
I pray it won't be long
Before we meet again
In the Cypress Hills

The moon was full so many years ago
In the Cypress Hills
When Sitting Bull held counsel with
Young Major Walsh

Two men of dignity
Spoke in the name of peace
But governments decreed
It could never be…oh will it ever be
In the Cypress Hills

I see the wild geese fly across the evening sky
In the Cypress Hills
I hear the cattle call and the coyote song
In the Cypress Hills

Don't you ever fear
We will still be here
No matter how things change
We remain the same
We are the Cypress Hills ♪

Epilogue

"….May you have fair winds
And blue sky…"

A Toast To Bob

One day
God spoke to Bob Wills –
"Bob…
Your time's up…
The gig's over"

Bob
Somewhat taken aback
Cleared his throat, doffed his hat
Looked upwards coyly
And said –

"Ah shucks Lord…surely not yet?"
Me and the Playboys' is really cookin'…
Why, this band is on fire
And we is goin' places –
even You never dreamed of
Top Forty, here we come!"

God, in the full realization He was addressing
The greatest Texas Swing player
He ever created
Looked down fondly upon his errant son
And with the gentle firmness of a daddy's hand
He majestically reminded Bob –

"Bob…
It's no longer a question
Of what Bob Wills
·It's now a matter of what God Wills
So come on up here and just chill"

236

So that's about the size of it
What life is all about
Follow your bliss, make hay in the sun
And then go on home...
When the Man with the Big Hat says –
the gig's over

Fair Winds, Blue Sky

May you have fair winds
And blue sky
From sunset through
Every new sunrise
Until you shall arrive
From yonder distant shore
Your sailor's dream
And your lover's prayer
Sailed safely home
To these arms of mine

(with FJS)

Life Is Poetry

Life is poetry
And how it rhymes
Is up to you –
That is when
You become
A poet

Sunset:
Nature's Closing Time

Words...
ideas, dreams, and memories
flowing from beginning to conclusion
as a creek finds its way to a river
and a river finds its way to the sea

Someone once said:
"You are both the picture and the artist...
the artist of your own personality"
And so perhaps we do what we will...
and become what we believe

And those who know and love the West...
cowboy, cowgirl, native, pioneer,
mystic, muse and urban refugee
find meaning in Mother Nature
and the vision to protect her

Imagination may be the greatest gift,
as Einstein once suggested...
but what better gift...it seems, than to see
Mother Nature as she really is...
watching an eagle fly...or a wild pony run!

Sunset...Nature's closing time...
time to let go...just unwind
into the colours, the quiet,
the peace of mind...
adios, my friend... goodnight

End Notes

SONGS in this book which can be heard on Saudara Music CD's:

Eagles – on CD 'Canadian Journey'...CD9901
Black Diamond Saloon...CD9901
Brightest Star...CD9901
Fraser Valley...CD9901
In Canada...CD9901
Mount Baker Serenade...CD9901
Red River Plains...CD9901
Alberta Serenade...CD9901
Rocky Mountain Time...CD9901
Saskatchewan...CD9901
River...CD9901
Corazon de Chihuahua – on CD
'Puppy Dog Heart'...CD0401
Mister (Mr) Moo...CD0401
Sea Shore Song – on CD
'Gentle Heart'... CD0402; & on CD0401
Thanks...CD0402

To order CD's, contact Saudara Music by mail, or visit www.marshallveal.net, or amazon.com

References:

Beal, Merrill D. (1981). I Will Fight No More Forever: Chief Joseph And The Nez Perce War. New York: Ballantine Books.

Brown, Dee (1971). Bury My Heart At Wounded Knee: An Indian History Of The American West.

New York: Holt, Rinehart and Winston.

Butala, Sharon (2005). LILAC MOON: Dreaming of the Real West. Toronto: HarperCollins PublishersLtd

Chief Seattle (1992). How Can One Sell The Air?: Chief Seattle's Vision. Summertown: Native Voices, The Book Publishing Company.

Flanagan, Thomas (1983). Louis 'David' Riel: Prophet of the New World. Halifax: Formac Publishing Company Limited.

Jones, Lonnie, in Taylor, Kim (Ed.), (2006). On The Trail: Day Planner 2006. Bragg Creek: Slidin' U Photography.

Keller, Betty C. (2000). Pender Harbour Cowboy: The Many Lives of Bertrand Sinclair. Victoria: Horsdal & Schubart Publishers Ltd.

MacEwan, Grant (1973). Sitting Bull: The Years in Canada. Edmonton: Hurtig Publishers.

Oliver, Mary (1990). HOUSE OF LIGHT. Boston: Beacon Press.

Quan, Holly (2003). Native Chiefs And Famous Metis: Leadership and Bravery in the Canadian West. Canmore: Altitude Publishing Canada Ltd.

Rodney, William (1996). KOOTENAI BROWN: Canada's Unknown Frontiersman. Nanoose Bay: Heritage House Publishing Company Ltd.

Also By The Author

recordings:

CANADIAN JOURNEY:
a songwriter's sketchbook
CD9901

PUPPY DOG HEART:
songs & lullabies for kids & other dreamers
CD0401

GENTLE HEART:
songs in the key of mindfulness
CD0402

visit www.marshallveal.net or amazon.com

About The Author

Marshall Veal's western roots go back to his great grandfather George Veal who, with three sons, including Marshall's grandad Austin Veal, emigrated from Liverpool and pioneered in Saskatchewan in 1885-1886 (they might be the original four Liverpool Lads...preceding The Beatles!). Must have been quite a time...with the recent Riel Rebellion and departure of Sitting Bull, the demise of the buffalo, uncertain politics, and those long prairie winters. It could fire the imagination of any would-be writer...as it apparently did.

With a prairie-bred father and an eastern poet mother, both musically inclined, something good was bound to happen.... Born after the war, and raised in Ontario's Ottawa Valley, with a few boyhood years in Manitoba's Red River country, Marshall developed an interest in western history and music, and talent for writing songs, poems, and playing guitar. Early musical forays included a duet with his sister Marianna (some critics say their version of Darcy Farrow is the best they've ever heard); later collaborations have followed, in folk, western, and music for children.

Marshall turned to his feeling for deeper roots in the West as a young man, moving West again after college. He lives in southern BC, where once upon a time he co-owned a co-operative cattle & farm operation. Along the way...he has worked in the health sciences, and may be one of the few western poets and pickers with a master's degree in psychology. Marshall has also travelled in the far east...and developed an abiding passion for the parallel wisdom and humour of both East and West. He has performed at Gatherings and Festivals in Europe and North America, and recorded three CD's of his own songs. Visit Marshall at www.marshallveal.net.

ISBN 1412059712

9 781412 059718